THE SOCCER
GOALKEEPING
HANDBOOK

3RD EDITION

THE SOCCER GOALKEEPING HANDBOOK

3RD EDITION

THE ESSENTIAL GUIDE FOR PLAYERS AND COACHES

ALEX WELSH

Note
While every effort has been made to ensure that the content of this book is as technically accurate and as sound as possible, neither the author nor the publishers can accept responsibility for any injury or loss sustained as a result of the use of this material.

Published by Bloomsbury Publishing Plc
50 Bedford Square
London WC1B 3DP
www.bloomsbury.com
Bloomsbury is a trade mark of Bloomsbury Publishing Plc

First edition 1998

Second edition 2004

Third edition 2014

Copyright © 1998, 2004, 2014 Alex Welsh

ISBN (print): 978-1-4081-9046-3

ISBN (ePdf): 978-1-4081-9215-3

ISBN (EPUB): 978-1-4729-0705-9

A CIP catalogue record for this book is available from the British Library.

Acknowledgements
Cover photograph © Daniel Ochoa Olza/AP/PA Images
Inside photographs, see page 172 for full picture credits
Design and Illustrations by Andrew Smith
Commissioned by Kirsty Schaper

This book is produced using paper that is made from wood grown in managed, sustainable forests. It is natural, renewable and recyclable. The logging and manufacturing processes conform to the environmental regulations of the country of origin.

Typeset in Adobe Caslon and Futura by Andrew Smith, UK

Printed and bound in China by Toppan Leefung printing

10 9 8 7 6 5 4 3 2

CONTENTS

PREFACE TO THE THIRD EDITION

I am very pleased to have the opportunity through this third edition to update the ideas and practices in this book. As the demands of the game are constantly changing it is vital that coaches ensure their work with players is relevant and keeps pace with current match requirements. After all, if coaching does not lead to improved match performance it is pointless.

In producing this book I would like to thank my good friends Pauline Cope (Charlton Athletic Ladies FC), Paul Heald (Wimbledon FC), Stuart Taylor (Arsenal FC), Emma Byrne (Arsenal Ladies FC) and Lee Butcher (Welling United FC) for their excellent contribution. The photo shoot was great fun and the standard of goalkeeping demonstrated in the impromptu training session at the end was breathtaking. I have coached all of them at various stages of their careers and they are all tremendous goalkeepers. I am grateful also to James Dalton (England futsal team) for his guidance on futsal goalkeeping techniques. I am also indebted to the many specialist coaches I have befriended over the years, in particular Perry Suckling for his ideas, generosity and integrity. My biggest vote of thanks goes to Bob Wilson who has exerted the greatest influence on my coaching career. As one of the world's leading authorities on the art of goalkeeping, Bob has been a tremendous source of knowledge and inspiration and taught me to always accentuate the positive. Thanks also to all the goalkeepers I have coached over the years. Each of them has presented a new challenge and helped me to improve my coaching effectiveness.

Finally, I am extremely grateful to my wife Maria for not only typing the original manuscript and curbing my verbosity but also for her continued support of my coaching work.

FOREWORD

The Soccer Goalkeeping Handbook is one of the best ever books written about the art of goalkeeping. It is certainly the most comprehensive. Whether you hold a burning ambition to play 'between the sticks', have a desire to coach and improve aspiring talent, or are simply curious about this most complex position, this is a manual that will broaden your knowledge, surprise you and best of all – inspire you. Having worked with Alex Welsh over many years, I am flattered to constantly hear myself talking within these pages. We have always shared ideas, thoughts and beliefs. Without sounding conceited, we believe 'our way' should be the benchmark adopted by national governing bodies.

The Soccer Goalkeeping Handbook is based on the best coaching principles and that is why I am so proud to be associated with it. Read this handbook, read it again, absorb it all and then, as a keeper, go out and improve your game or, as a coach, blend the best of these ideals with the best of you. All you need to know about modern-day goalkeeping is contained within these pages. Simply adapt them to your own style, strengths and personality.

Bob Wilson
Arsenal FC and Scotland
Arsenal FC Head Goalkeeping Coach
Sports Broadcaster

HOW TO USE THIS BOOK

This book is written with the needs of the player, coach and parent in mind. For the player it might be affirmation or clarification on a particular point; for the coach it might be ideas on developing a technical or tactical theme; and for the parent it might be simple guidance. Essentially the book is concerned with improving a goalkeeper's match performance and helping the reader to become a more effective keeper.

The book is divided into three main parts. Part I identifies the key elements of goalkeeping success, which in turn provide a focus for the various practices later in the book. It also explores what makes a successful coach and offers advice on planning individual sessions and programmes as well as developing the keeper's physical, mental, technical and social strengths. The chapter on preparing to play and train highlights the importance of being mentally and physically ready for optimum performance. The final chapter in this section describes the fundamentals of goalkeeping emphasising that a mastery of the basics is essential for later success.

Part II provides a range of progressive practices covering the five goalkeeping roles of shot stopping, fielding crosses, dealing with through balls, distribution and organising the defence. Each role is broken down into individual themes which reflect situations that the keeper might encounter during a game. Each theme has a number of realistic and relevant practices attached to it; and with every practice there is an explanation of the assessment, decision and technique involved accompanied by key coaching points. Based on the goalkeeper's needs, the coach can then select those practices that are most appropriate. Where applicable, a description of common faults that the coach might encounter when covering a particular theme is provided.

Part III provides tips on goalkeeping in futsal and 5-a-side formats. It also covers physical conditioning for the goalkeeper by providing exercises aimed at improving strength, speed, mobility and agility. Finally the book concludes with the 10 Golden Rules of Goalkeeping.

INTRODUCTION

Contrary to the popular theory, goalkeepers are not mad, they are just a breed apart.

Without doubt, the goalkeeper is the most important position in the soccer team and is the only position stipulated in the laws of the game. Nearly every senior club now has a qualified specialist goalkeeping coach. The performance of the goalkeeper can make or break a team, and it is no coincidence that the most successful clubs have the best keepers. The 'mad' label reflects the individual nature of the job and the lengths to which the keeper will go to protect his goal. Most of the goalkeepers I have met place a clean sheet before personal safety and, therefore, those who do not share the obsession are driven to question their sanity.

This common purpose has led to the development of a genuine camaraderie between goalkeepers. It is often said that they are the keenest of rivals but the best of friends, and this is why people often refer to the 'goalkeeper's union' when keepers stick up for each other. After a match goalkeepers often get together to chat about aspects of their craft in a way that outfield players do not.

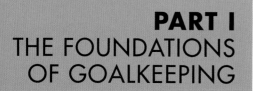

PART I
THE FOUNDATIONS
OF GOALKEEPING

1

WHAT MAKES A TOP GOALKEEPER?

Soccer is a team game until the goalkeeper makes a mistake and then it becomes an individual sport.

While a striker will be measured by the positive things he does, a goalkeeper will be judged on the mistakes he makes, and this is why the position of goalkeeper is the most pressurised on the field and often the loneliest. All players will make errors, but the keeper's usually result in a goal conceded. Once he manages to keep his mistakes to a minimum and prove his reliability, his work will be measured by the important saves he makes. Good goalkeepers put their mistakes behind them and learn from the experience. One mistake does not make a bad goalkeeper, or one save a good goalkeeper.

Identifying what makes a top goalkeeper in the modern game is more than assessing their ability to save shots and take crosses. Approximately 60–70 per cent of the keeper's work will be taken up by what I call gamecraft – distribution, receiving back passes and dealing with through balls. The goalkeeping art can be likened to a present where the wrapping paper (what the observer first sees) is how well he deals with these gamecraft elements. If the keeper is deficient in these areas there may be no further interest in finding out what is inside the wrapping paper, namely the ability to save shots and deal with crosses.

Goalkeepers who have reached the top have benefited from three key factors encapsulated in the following:

> Natural ability/talent
> +
> Attitude
> +
> Opportunity
> =
> Reaching the top

Are top goalkeepers born or made? This question has vexed coaches for many years and there is no simple answer. Given the correct conditions, cream will rise to the top, but talent can be inhibited by low motivation levels, poor coaching and a lack of exposure to challenging match experiences.

THE QUALITIES OF THE GOALKEEPER

Natural ability/talent

It can be difficult to define natural ability, but when I see a goalkeeper for the first time, I assess how comfortable he looks in the position and how difficult it is for the opposition to score. A naturally talented goalkeeper has a combination of outstanding technical, physical and mental attributes. What stands out for me is how well he handles the ball (as this is the equivalent to an outfield player's touch) and how well he moves as this will determine the extent to which he manages to be in the right place at the right time. While the capacity to move with great pace and control is critical – as speed in all its forms (off and across the ground, of reactions and of thought) characterises the great goalkeeper – technical mastery across the five goalkeeping roles is essential for those performing at elite level since any weakness can be ruthlessly exposed by the opposition. Thankfully from the coaching perspective natural ability can be developed and, given the appropriate learning environment, flourish.

Competitiveness

Good players do not become great without committing themselves wholeheartedly to improving their craft and ultimately their match performance. This inner drive is easy to detect in goalkeepers – how much does he want to prevent the ball going into the net? The extent to which the player does not want to be beaten will determine how hard he will work to polish his strengths and minimise his weaknesses. This, of course, will involve some degree of self-analysis, and it is imperative that the keeper is totally honest with himself. Another feature of a successful goalkeeper is their ability to cope with the pressure of making mistakes. All keepers make errors but the best have the mental toughness not to let these undermine their confidence or concentration levels and not to allow one mistake to lead to another.

Soccer intelligence

Since the goalkeeper is expected to play virtually as an additional outfield player, either to patrol the area behind the defence or to initiate attacks, it is essential that he is able to read the game. He should be able to support this understanding with sound decision making. The ability to consistently make good decisions usually distinguishes the confident, positive player from the nervous, unreliable one.

Presence

The truly great goalkeepers appear to have an aura about them and an ability to fill up the goal. While they may be feeling very nervous inwardly, they appear to play with such authority and confidence that they inspire and influence those around them. The top performer remains composed even under extreme pressure and his decision making and technique are unaffected by external factors. It is important that young goalkeepers learn to develop this on-field personality, a determination to be in control of, rather than be controlled by, the situation.

Making the most of match opportunities

Appropriate match experience is essential if the goalkeeper is to develop in the right way. Ideally the player should not be performing at a standard where he is too comfortable. If his potential is to be fulfilled, the demands placed on him should be challenging. This may involve playing promising youngsters above and, on the odd occasion, below their age group. The coach must remember that actual match practice is the richest learning environment. Eventually every player will find his own level but for the up and coming young goalkeeper presented with his breakthrough match he must be ready to make the most of the opportunity and move up the pecking order.

SCOUTING YOUNG GOALKEEPERS

While identifying the best player in a match is relatively straightforward, assessing potential is not so easy and requires an experienced eye. Much, of course, will depend on the scout's expectations, which will be influenced by long-term player development principles and specifically by:

- The level for which the scout is recruiting. In other words, how does the player in question compare with the goalkeepers already in the team or squad?
- Their age.
- Their experience.
- The level at which they currently play.

The best scouts do their homework and know what they are looking for before going on a scouting trip. They should watch the player over a number of matches as the degree to which the keeper is called into action will be out of his control and be determined by the quality of his own team and the opposition. A scout should arrive early and watch the goalkeeper warm up as that will provide an insight into his physical, technical, mental and social attributes. Generally speaking the whole is greater than the sum of the parts and following the observation, the scout should be able to compile a list of 'wow factors' that set the keeper apart from the rest. These factors may be found in the following 'four corner' checklist.

Physical

Physique is important when scouting a more mature goalkeeper, but when looking at eight-year-olds for instance it is less of a factor. However, good spring and speed off and across the ground are essential raw ingredients.

Technical

Handling, positioning, shot stopping, distribution and reading the game are all key components underpinning successful performance.

Mental

Bravery and a willingness to go where he might get hurt should be in the keeper's DNA but mental courage and the ability to recover from mistakes are just as crucial. Competitiveness and concentration are also vital ingredients in the top goalkeeper's make-up.

Social

Does the keeper have a presence and impose himself on situations rather than allow himself to be controlled by others? Does he look at home in the goal? Does he present a formidable barrier when the opposition attacks?

Within professional clubs there should be close dialogue between the recruitment and coaching staff so that the scouts are looking for the same characteristics that the coaches are hoping to develop. It does help the process if the scouts have a clear idea of what the relevant benchmarks are at the various age groups. The following represents a range of expectations at a typical English Premier League Academy:

FUNDAMENTAL PHASE
9–10 year olds

1 Natural movement skills.

2 Hand eye coordination.

3 Athleticism.

4 Basic mastery of handling and diving techniques.

5 Natural enthusiasm and love for the game.

6 Willingness to learn and the ability to absorb new information.

DEVELOPMENT PHASE
11–12 year olds

1 Good movement off and across the ground.

2 Mastery of basic shot-stopping techniques.

3 Understanding of positioning.

4 A range of effective throwing techniques.

5 Ability to cope with the back pass.

6 Starting to make good decisions.

7 A strong competitive streak.

13–14 year olds

1 Speed around the goal.

2 Agility.

3 Well-developed shot-stopping techniques.

4 Understanding of counter-attacking.

5 A willingness to deal with high crosses.

6 Appropriate use of communication skills.

7 Mental strength becomes more noticeable.

15–16 year olds

1 Presence.

2 Speed, agility, power.

3 Obvious key strengths.

4 Full tactical awareness.

5 Ability to deal with a range of crosses.

6 Good reader of through balls.

7 Good organiser.

8 Full understanding of the requirements of the position.

9 High levels of concentration.

PROFESSIONAL PHASE
17–21 year olds

1 High levels of balance, coordination, power and speed.

2 Very well-developed techniques for shot stopping and dealing with crosses.

3 Full understanding of the goalkeeper's contribution to team play.

4 Well-developed gamecraft.

5 Decisive.

6 High levels of consistency.

7 Strong personality.

8 Excellent levels of concentration.

9 Highly competitive.

10 Mentally tough.

COACHING GOALKEEPERS

If learning is a journey, coaching is the map

Learning by trial and error can be risky, in that it can lead to the development of bad habits and faulty technique. The good coach will take a long-term view, ensuring that the player's game is built on sound fundamentals rather than what works in the short term. In addition to facilitating learning and improving performance, he will also imbue the player with a love for the game and a determination to be better. Coaches of teams at all levels need to be well equipped to look after their goalkeepers. It has been said that it takes a goalkeeper to coach a goalkeeper, and there is some truth in this. Aside from the technical input, the coach must understand what it is like to play in that position. However, you can be the greatest goalkeeper in the world and yet be ineffective as a coach. This is because the whole purpose of coaching is not to demonstrate personal prowess, but to bring out the best in others.

While I fully subscribe to the need for specialist qualifications for goalkeeping coaches, it must not result in the team coaches thinking that the goalkeeping role is someone else's responsibility. There are too many coaches whose knowledge and understanding of the position is very limited, and as a consequence their ability to influence and inform the whole team is adversely affected. It should be mandatory for all senior coaches to have their national association's basic goalkeeping coaching award. In a similar vein I believe that specialist coaches should see themselves as teachers of the game first and goalkeeping coaches second. In the modern game where the keeper often operates as the eleventh player, it is very important that his coach understands the whole game and not just what happens in the goal area. Given the individual nature of goalkeeping coaching, where the keepers often train separately, there is a danger that keepers become isolated from the main group. The coach should be guided by the maxim that the goalkeeper is a part of and not apart from the team. Involving

the keeper in the squad development of possession practices will assist the keeper's social integration as well as improving his outfield skills.

It is often said that soccer is a game of varying opinions, and this probably explains the lack of a consistent approach when it comes to goalkeeping coaching. In some quarters technical sessions are based on making multiple saves where the goalkeeper faces a barrage of shots in a matter of seconds or in others where the keeper has to jump over an obstacle before making the save. However, how often would the keeper be called upon to make a quadruple save in a game, or leap over a hurdle in the goalmouth? My approach is game related, and when designing practices for the keeper I am guided by the following:

- Is it realistic? Does it happen in a game?
- Is it relevant? Does it improve technical development and decision making?
- Is it appropriate? Is the practice suitable for the age, experience and ability of the goalkeeper?

The perceptive coach will be able to observe his goalkeeper's match performance and isolate areas that require special attention during training and then organise practices that recreate the same picture, problem and pressure. By facing every given situation in training the keeper will be able to recognise when something very similar happens in a game and hopefully be able to deal with it. Coaching based on this principle, tailored to the individual needs of the goalkeeper, will help him to grow in confidence and competence.

Furthermore, as the game and the demands placed on players are constantly changing, it is vital that coaches move with the times and meet the challenges of the modern game. Over the last ten years modifications to the laws of the game, team tactics, the aerodynamics of the balls and improvements to playing surfaces have affected the position of goalkeeper more than any other. There is little doubt that these factors coupled with 24/7 media coverage mean that the pressure on the current elite goalkeepers is greater than it ever has been, and this presents a special challenge to their coaches.

In looking at the performance of the coach, his performance can be assessed on the degree to which he achieves the seven 'I's:

- IGNITING a passion and enthusiasm for the game.

- INFORMING players through the transference of appropriate pieces of technical and tactical knowledge.

- INCREASING the players' physical capabilities.

- INSTRUCTING players on the importance of sound decision making.

- INFLUENCING players' attitudes to training and matches.

- INSPIRING a positive mentality where nothing less than the players' best will do.

- IMPROVING match performance which is the ultimate coaching aim.

THE QUALITIES OF THE COACH

In identifying what sets the top coach apart from the rest there are five key areas that should be considered – philosophy, knowledge, observational, organisational and communication skills.

Philosophy

In assessing coaching effectiveness there is little doubt that the philosophy of the coach plays a vital role in encouraging the goalkeeper to perform to an optimal level and to play without fear. Attitudes are contagious and the coach must ensure that his attitude is worth catching. Choosing the correct coaching philosophy is absolutely critical as it underpins a coach's approach to training and matches. Many less experienced coaches are obsessed with the content of sessions without realising that how they broach the task of bringing out the best in their players is just as important as what they actually do with them. It is said that players might forget what the coach looks like or what he said to them but what they never forget is how he made them feel. Therefore it is crucial that the coach understands what defines him as a coach.

In determining the ideal approach it might be helpful to consider the acronym PELE

Positiveness. Players respond much more readily to a coach who is pleased to be there so his priority should be to create a positive learning environment. Instilling a 'can do' mentality rather than a fear of failure greatly enhances the players' chances of fulfilling their potential. Accentuating the positive by building on what the keeper can do is far more powerful than focusing on deficiencies.

Enthusiasm. Since enjoyment is the first aim of every training session the coach must commit himself fully to ensuring that his players are maximally involved, have fun and learn from the experience. Letting the players practise without constant interference will also contribute to the players' enjoyment.

Leadership. As a role model the coach has to ensure that the example he sets is worthy of emulation. The coach is a very influential person, particularly in the lives of young players, and he must take this responsibility seriously. Setting the highest standards of himself before demanding them of others will help set the correct tone.

Empowerment. Good coaching is about giving players the confidence to make decisions under pressure. To achieve this, the coach must first give his players the knowledge and the opportunity to practise decision making without fear of admonishment. Players who are constantly dominated by the coach will be frightened to make their own informed decisions.

Knowledge of the subject

While it is not essential that the coach has been a goalkeeper, it is essential that he has a good knowledge of the subject matter because the consequences of imparting incorrect information could spell disaster. The demands of the game are evolving constantly, so a coach never stops learning. The good coach has an obligation to maintain an open and enquiring mind and must move with the times.

Understanding of his players

If the coach is to apply his knowledge and experience successfully, he must understand how players learn. He must also be aware of his keeper's capabilities and how to bring out the best in him. A working knowledge of long-term player development along with the ability to transfer knowledge in bite-sized chunks commensurate with the level of his players will help the coach work effectively across the age groups.

Observational skills

One of the coach's greatest tools is the power of observation. In order to minimise the goalkeeper's weaknesses, the coach should be able to diagnose key faults in the player's performance. These defects may be related to technical deficiencies, poor assessment, incorrect decisions, negative starting positions, poor physical fitness or lack of confidence.

Organisational ability

Having identified the fault, the coach should be able to set up a coaching situation that affords concentrated practice on a particular aspect. To do this he must be aware of the sequential nature of coaching and start at a level where the keeper can achieve success. For example, if a goalkeeper is having difficulty in dealing with high crosses during games, it would be inadvisable to begin the practice with the penalty area crowded with players. It would benefit both the player and the coach to commence with an unopposed practice where the keeper could be observed fielding crosses in isolation.

Once satisfied that the basic technique is sound and that the keeper is achieving success, by introducing defenders and then attackers, the coach can assess his player's decision making and technique under more realistic circumstances. At each stage of the progression it is essential that the keeper is regularly experiencing success before moving on to a more challenging situation. Hopefully, by the end of the session the goalkeeper will be performing effectively under simulated match conditions.

Goalkeeping coaching is not solely about exercises designed to have the keeper diving everywhere at great speed. There is a place for pressure training as part of the conditioning and fitness process, but there are very few occasions during actual matches when the keeper is faced with a barrage of shots. More importantly, the coach must remember that technique breaks down when fatigue sets in. If the practice is intended to improve technique, then the keeper should be allowed to recover between each save. Forcing the player to react in an unrealistic way might result in a rushed technique and, ultimately, in the development of bad habits.

Poor feeding starves the practice, and care should be taken that the quality of service is maintained throughout the session. The keeper should be faced with shots which he has a realistic chance of saving. He will learn very little, and probably become demoralised very quickly, if every shot ends up in the back of the net. Similarly, if the service is too easy and does not stretch the goalkeeper, limited progress will be made.

On a cautionary note, it should not be assumed that all finishing practice designed for strikers is valuable to goalkeepers. In the same way that playing a round of golf is not necessarily putting practice, the organisation and demands of the exercise should be tailored to the needs of the players it is supposed to benefit. Often finishing practices involve unopposed rapid-fire close-range strikes, giving the keeper no respite and little chance of improving his shot-stopping technique.

Communication skills

Throughout the coaching programme, the coach should adapt his style to suit the circumstances and to keep his players stimulated. On some occasions he might use a command method and tell the player what to do, while on others he might use a question and answer approach, or even guide his player towards certain outcomes. Whatever style is used, the coaching points should be clear, concise, relevant and above all tailored

to the level of understanding of the keeper. Where appropriate, these factors should be accompanied by a demonstration, because a visual explanation can speak a thousand words.

THE PSYCHOLOGY OF GOALKEEPING COACHING – THE SEVEN Cs

Goalkeeping is like walking a tightrope without a safety net, so the key to being successful requires great mental strength.

Goalkeeping, in common with all the other outfield positions involves the following process in virtually every situation:

> **Assessment (of danger/opportunity)**
> ⌄
> **Decision (on the best course of action)**
> ⌄
> **Application of the appropriate technique (to solve the problem/take advantage of the situation)**

However, for the goalkeeper there is no margin for error. For the forward, midfielder or defender a loss of possession is not necessarily game changing, but for the keeper an error can spell disaster for the team. Therefore functioning effectively in this pressurised situation requires a strong mentality. It is not surprising to learn that the best goalkeeping coaches are great psychologists. So what are the key elements of mental strength? And what can the goalkeeper and his coach do to improve them?

Confidence

By far and away the most critical psychological attribute is confidence, as it is the glue that holds the keeper's game together. Confidence comes before competence in any sporting endeavour, and without it even the most gifted performer can look like a novice. For the keeper, it helps him to make positive decisions and to cope with pressure. Confidence also enhances consistency since it assists the goalkeeper to execute previously learned skills and techniques. It is about self-belief: knowing that you will be able to handle certain situations when they arise. Above all, it is about not letting mistakes undermine your faith in your own ability. Unfortunately, confidence levels are at the mercy of events or comments from others, and unless continually topped up, they can drop to a point where performance is impaired.

How the keeper can increase and sustain his confidence

Adopting a philosophical attitude to mistakes combined with the constant polishing of strengths and improvement of weaknesses via correct practice will help increase self-belief. All keepers make mistakes but the best make the fewest. They might strive for perfection but they do not expect it – at least not every time! They have strategies for dealing with mistakes while realising that they can only deal with the 'here and now' and should force themselves not to dwell on mistakes because this will damage concentration.

Before matches the keeper should visualise himself playing well, and prepare physically and mentally for the game ahead. Desire is positive and fear is negative if not managed properly. While fear of failure can be a good thing in that it prevents the onset of complacency, all players should begin each game and training session in a positive frame of mind.

How the coach can increase and sustain the keeper's confidence

In training, the coach and the keeper should agree to work on areas that need attention as well as staging regular practice on the basics of head, hands and feet. Mastery of the basic skills and techniques will give any athlete an excellent foundation on which to build his performance, and goalkeepers are no different. The coach should always try to accentuate the positive and be quick to recognise progress. Coaching tricks of the trade, such as finishing every practice on a save, do wonders for self-esteem. By facing every given situation in training, the keeper will not be 'phased' when faced by similar circumstances during a game.

The coach should also work on his players' mental toughness and help them to cope with the pressures of playing in a position where one mistake can result in a goal conceded, and ultimately, possible defeat. This psychological function is, without doubt, one of the most difficult aspects of goalkeeping. The coach will be the first person to whom the goalkeeper turns when things are not going well, and the coach must have the answers. When form drops, confidence is affected. The coach not only has to help rectify any tactical or technical deficiencies but also bolster self-belief. In short, the coach must not lose faith, even if the player does.

Concentration

Lapses in concentration are often the reason why mistakes occur so it is vital that the keeper stays in the game at all times. I often use the light switch analogy to explain concentration to young players – if you walk into a dark room it is highly likely that you will walk into things but if you switch on the light you are aware of all the dangers and pitfalls.

It only takes a split-second to let in a goal, so if the keeper 'switches off' during a game, the result could be catastrophic. He must live every second of the game and be ready for any eventuality. Unlike outfield players, the keeper cannot go off in pursuit of the ball, searching for action. The extent to which he is occupied depends on how successful the opposition is in getting the ball close to his goal.

Generally speaking, it is easier to perform effectively when constantly involved in the action rather than when called upon to make a save only once in a while. When inactive for long spells, it is essential that the goalkeeper maintains a high level of concentration and tries to involve himself in the game as much as possible. Even when play is in the opponent's half he can be constantly adjusting his position ready for a quick breakaway and, of course, he can keep in touch with play by being a source of information and encouragement for the defenders in front of him. The enemy of concentration is complacency so the key to success is to take nothing for granted and be primed for action at all times. This means treating every shot with respect and being prepared for the worst from teammates and the best from opponents.

Mistakes can result in a loss of concentration while the player replays the error in his mind. Trigger words such as 'next save' can help the keeper to focus on what is in front of him and to get on with the remainder of the game. Goalkeepers make mistakes in training so this tactic of homing in on the next save can help develop a strong mindset and improve concentration levels.

Competitiveness

All goalkeepers should be determined not to be beaten, and if they are, it should be a momentary personal tragedy. Unless the keeper is prepared to fully commit himself (including risking personal safety) in order to prevent a goal, he will never be successful. A strong competitive streak will result in a positive approach to the game and will boost confidence. Indeed, the manner in which a keeper performs is just as important as his physical characteristics. If the goalkeeper believes he is a giant who has to dominate his area, he will play like one, irrespective of his size. Like confidence, this will to win is infectious and a keeper can inspire his defenders with the same determination to keep his goal intact.

It is important that players are also competitive in training because it is not a quality that can be turned on like a tap just for matches. The determination not to concede a goal must be a permanent feature of the keeper's make-up. This commitment to winning will result in a conscientious approach to training and will ensure that areas of weakness are given sufficient attention.

Commitment

If any player is to realise his true potential then he must commit himself fully to improving his craft. This entails adopting a lifestyle that gives him the edge as well as total application in training and matches. Every day that he arrives for training it should be with the ambition of becoming a better player because of the experience. 'Nothing less than my best' should be his maxim and this attitude of always giving 100 per cent should be carried over into matches. This approach will help sustain high levels of concentration and eventually lead to a consistent level of performance.

Composure

The ability to keep your head when everyone else is losing theirs is a vital quality, since the goalkeeping position is a highly pressurised one. As the lynchpin of the defence, the keeper cannot allow himself to panic when under stress. Other players will look to him to set the tone so it is important that he exudes a calm authority. Goalkeepers who constantly harangue the defence run the risk of losing concentration and alienating colleagues. There is a place for a justified reprimand, but it should be employed sparingly.

Furthermore, if the keeper is to be an effective organiser of the defence he has to remain cool, calm and collected even in the most chaotic moments when his goal is under severe pressure.

Courage

There are two types of courage, one physical and the other mental. There are bound to be occasions during matches when the keeper, in an attempt to prevent a goal, risks injury. These situations demand raw courage inspired by the desire not to be beaten. However, if the keeper applies the correct technique and commits himself fully to the physical confrontation, serious injury should seldom result. In any case, most keepers feel more pain when the ball hits the back of the net than when taking a physical knock. Often the keeper's courage can turn a game, especially in 1 v 1 situations. The coach can recreate situations where the keeper has to 'go where it hurts' so that he develops the appropriate techniques and overcomes any fears.

Courage of a different sort is the mental strength to make crucial decisions. For instance, when conditions are muddy and the opposition aggressive, it is easier to stay on the line than to come for a high cross. However, the keeper has to back his ability and make the correct decision. This mental courage will be tested to the full during those times when confidence is low and negative tendencies predominate over the positive. Form will only be rediscovered by conquering fear and making the correct decisions.

Control

The best goalkeepers dominate their area with their performance and presence and this gives them a large degree of control. Like the conductor of an orchestra they organise the defenders in front of them to protect their goal. To exercise this control the goalkeeper must develop an understanding of the roles and responsibilities of his teammates so that he can give them the correct information. He must then develop an on-pitch personality that allows him to take charge of the situation and couple this with an ability to communicate effectively and efficiently. The coach can help by developing the keeper's leadership skills and by providing a vocabulary list of helpful phrases.

PLANNING, PREPARING, DELIVERING AND EVALUATING COACHING PROGRAMMES AND SESSIONS

3

Fuelling a love for the game and fulfilling potential should be the key drivers of any coaching programme

PLANNING PROGRAMMES

In planning any session, programme or syllabus the coach has to relate the content to the needs of the player. For the senior goalkeeper, aside from pre-season training or rehabilitation after an injury lay-off, the priority will be on preparing him for the next game and ensuring that he is in the best physical, mental and technical shape to produce a top performance. On the other hand, for young goalkeepers the focus will not be on immediate goals but instead on longer-term objectives. Many sports now take this longer view, sometimes known as long-term athlete development, when attempting to fulfil the potential of younger players. This model, which is based on specific stages of development roughly correlating to chronological age, helps the coach adopt an approach where the intensity and complexity of the session are appropriate to:

- General physical, intellectual and emotional maturation levels.
- Playing experience.
- Physical capabilities such as speed, power, endurance and flexibility.
- Technical expertise.
- Tactical understanding.

Development phases

In the academy structure within professional clubs in England there are three broad phases:

1 Fundamental Development Phase – 9 to 11 years

2 Youth Development Phase – 12 to 16 years

3 Professional Development Phase – 16 to 21 years

Aim of the programme

Categorising player development into these stages helps the coach to tailor his methods according to where an individual is on their way to realising their potential. The aim should be to help every player be the best that they can be, both as a goalkeeper and as a young person.

In order to achieve this, the coach should ensure where possible that every session:

- Is enjoyable and personally rewarding.
- Provides optimal levels of involvement and practice.
- Is stimulating and promotes learning.

Programme philosophy

The most effective way of achieving these three goals is for the coach to have a consistent player-centred approach that can be neatly summarised in the acronym GK GOALS.

Generate a positive learning environment.

Keep things in perspective, take the long-term view and do not rush to judge.

Games programme tailored to individual needs so players may play in, above or below their age group.

Organise game-like practices that are realistic, relevant and appropriate, and are based on actual match scenarios.

Accentuate the positive and build on what players can do.

Let players practise without the fear of failure being an inhibiting factor.

Set the highest standards of everyone involved in the learning environment.

Key development areas

In planning any programme the coach must have a clear idea of what he wants to develop. Using the English FA's Four Corner model (physical, technical/tactical, psychological/mental and social/personality) will help to focus the coach's mind.

For the goalkeeper the four corners might include those in the table on the right.

Physical	Psychological/Mental
Agility	Presence
Balance	Confidence
Coordination	Concentration
Speed	Competitiveness
Strength	Composure
Power	Courage
Endurance	Consistency
	Dealing with mistakes
Social/Personality	**Technical/Tactical**
Humility	The basics
Honesty	Shot stopping
Being a team player	Positioning
Living and behaving as an elite athlete	Saving on the move
	Dealing with the unexpected
Taking responsibility	Saving in 1 v 1 situations
Respectful of others	Reaction saves
	Saving penalties
	Distribution
	Dealing with the back pass
	Dealing with through balls
	Organising the defence

Technical syllabus

The key technical/tactical development areas form the basis of the coaching syllabus and reflect the five goalkeeping roles of: shot stopping; fielding crosses; distribution; dealing with through balls; and organising the defence. The programme below is based on a ten-week cycle, covering each of the technical themes listed above. For each week there is a different theme delivered within two or three 75-minute sessions. Each theme is broken down into a range of practices, the complexity and intensity of which is related to the age, experience and ability of the players concerned. Players attend sessions in two or three year age bands so that the ability range across the group is not too great. As distribution is such an integral part of the goalkeeper's job, throwing or kicking drills appear in most sessions as either introductory or cool-down activities.

Coaching cycle

Week 1	The basics – footwork and handling
Week 2	Shot stopping (including saving penalties)
Week 3	Positioning
Week 4	Saving on the move
Week 5	Dealing with the unexpected
Week 6	Reaction saves
Week 7	Saving in 1 v 1 situations
Week 8	Dealing with crosses
Week 9	Distribution and dealing with the back pass
Week 10	Dealing with through balls and organising the defence at set pieces

Planning goalkeeping camps

Having worked with the peerless Bob Wilson Goalkeeping Schools for seventeen years, I know what a great experience they can be for young people. Even now, over twenty years later, I have adults recalling how Bob's camps were one of the most enjoyable and rewarding weeks of their lives! His school was characterised by charismatic leadership from Bob, inspirational coaches, generous coach–player ratios, a varied and exciting programme and access to good quality facilities and equipment.

In planning a camp programme, care needs to be taken in how the days are organised because goalkeeping practices can be very physically demanding. In the example provided overleaf, the days are broken down into five sessions with the theory/DVD session taking place at lunchtime. These sessions can be used to either consolidate the previous session or preview the next one.

Each session focuses on a different technical theme with each day concluding with some element of distribution. 2 v 2 is a great way to finish the day as the competitive element brings out the best in the goalkeepers. The final day concentrates on applying the techniques and skills learned during the week to game related situations or small-sided games.

Day	Session 1	Session 2	Session 3	Session 4	Session 5
MONDAY	Ball familiarity	The Basics: Footwork Handling	Review/Preview DVD	The Basics: Diving techniques	Distribution: Javelin/sling 2 v 2
TUESDAY	Shot stopping	Positioning	Review/Preview DVD	Saving on the move	Distribution: Overarm 2 v 2
WEDNESDAY	Unorthodox saves	Reaction saves	Review/Preview DVD	Saving in 1 v 1 situations	Distribution: Drill/wedge/drive Heading game
THURSDAY	Dealing with through balls	Dealing with crosses	Review/Preview DVD	Dealing with back passes	Distribution: Kicking from hands Saving penalties
FRIDAY	SSG Shot stopping	SSG Counter Attacking	Camp review DVD	SSG Dealing with back passes	Presentation

PLANNING AND PREPARING SESSIONS

One of the most undisputed maxims in sports coaching is: 'Fail to prepare – prepare to fail'. For all coaches, planning is a vital part of any effective coaching session. Good planning will often pre-empt problems and help the coach to achieve his objectives.

In considering coaching objectives the following acronym is useful:

Purpose

Activity

Safety

Satisfaction

Every session should have a point to it and this objective should relate to some longer-term aim. Furthermore, it is of particular value to involve the players in goal setting because, by placing them at the centre of the learning experience, their motivation is increased.

In order to provide opportunities to improve techniques and decision making, it is crucial that there is plenty of activity. However, it would be prudent to remember that it is correct practice that makes perfect. Furthermore, it goes without saying that the safety of the goalkeeper is of paramount importance. The coach should ensure that all factors relating to the facility, weather conditions, equipment and demands of the session do not put the players' safety at undue risk.

Playing soccer should be enjoyable, so sessions should be both challenging and varied. Satisfaction is further enhanced when the player can see that he is improving.

Planning considerations

The content and delivery of any coaching programme or session will be determined by a number of factors, some related to the goalkeeper's personal needs and others influenced by environmental circumstances.

Size

When planning any session, the physical characteristics of the players must be considered. The content of the session must relate to the needs of the goalkeepers involved. For example, it would be unrealistic to cover the high cross with ten-year-olds because they are not physically capable of dealing with them and are very rarely faced with the situation during matches.

Age

While grouping players according to age is often the most expedient method, it can be misleading since adolescents of the same age can be up to four years apart in physical development. Grouping by size, experience and ability might prove more appropriate.

Experience

All sessions should be designed to expand on what has already been learned. This is crucial if the keeper is to remain motivated and challenged. As with physical size, experience is a better yardstick than age.

Ability

The level of ability, coupled with experience, will determine how sophisticated the coaching programme should be. It is imperative that the content of the sessions challenges the players so that improvement takes place.

Group size

In aiming for high quality goalkeeping sessions, low coach/player ratios are vital. By working with smaller groups, the coach will be able to make optimum use of space and equipment and, more importantly, give each player their fullest attention.

Group range

It is very difficult to coach a group of players where there is a wide discrepancy in size, experience and ability. If it is not possible to work with a homogeneous group, the coach should set a range of tasks suited to the individual needs of the players.

Place in the syllabus

The content of the session will reflect where the coach is in the overall programme of work as indicated in the coaching cycle described earlier.

Responding to previous/forthcoming matches

Any coach should be responsive to problems that his players are encountering during matches, and if a goalkeeper is experiencing difficulties in a particular aspect there ought to be the opportunity to rectify any faults and allay any fears. Conversely the team may be scheduled to compete in a forthcoming match against opposition whose style of play warrants special preparation.

Weather

If the prevailing weather conditions are extreme they will have an impact on the content and intensity of the session. In very hot conditions the coach needs to consider giving the players more to drink and more rest breaks than normal. On the other hand if it is very cold, the coach will need to keep his players on the move in order to retain their body temperature. High winds will also have an impact on the session content as they will affect the quality of the service.

Facility

During the winter months it is often not possible to work in ideal conditions. Generally, at this time, the keeper has to work under floodlights on artificial surfaces where there may be less space available. Third generation rubber crumb artificial pitches are now widely used and can provide a more reliable surface than frozen or muddy goalmouths.

Safety

The safety of all players is of paramount importance and the coach should take appropriate steps to ensure that the facility, equipment, session structure and content do not jeopardise the keepers' health.

Quality of service

In order to provide plenty of touches, many practices are conducted in pairs with the keepers serving each other. Poor feeding starves the practice, so it is vital that the goalkeepers are capable of a good standard of service.

Structuring and delivering sessions

Having reflected on the planning considerations, the coach should now prepare the session. The following structure is recommended.

Warm-up

The warm-up, which helps the body to gradually adjust from a resting state to an optimal level of readiness to train or play, has three main objectives:

* To raise the heart rate so that the base body temperature is increased.
* To warm the muscles, tendons and ligaments, and to stretch them to their working length, to reduce the chance of soft tissue injury.
* To mentally prepare the player for the task in hand and to practise some of the techniques that may be required.

Warm-up exercises with the ball should always involve ball familiarity and distribution drills so that the goalkeeper becomes equally comfortable with his hands and his feet.

Explanation of session objectives

It is important that the coach shares the session objectives with his players as this will help them to appreciate the relevance of the various practices and assist in the learning process. The objectives should relate to physical, technical, tactical, and psychological and social improvements. As the coaching of goalkeepers is usually conducted in small groups, sometimes even one-to-one, there is more of a dialogue between players and coach than is the case with outfield colleagues. Therefore, it is relatively easy for the coach to tailor the session to meet individual needs.

In planning training programmes, the aims should be SMART.

Specific

Measurable

Agreed

Realistic

Time related

Session objectives will be determined by a combination of:

* Long-term programme goals.
* Performances in recent matches.
* Specific preparation for forthcoming matches.

Prior knowledge of likely session demands and expectations will help the goalkeeper to place the practices into context and to focus on each aspect.

Technical theme

Every session should include work on polishing technique. Following the ball familiarity and ball control/passing exercises included in the warm-up, the goalkeeper should always have the opportunity to hone his handling and footwork skills. The development of technique is dependent upon correct practice so it is imperative that the keeper receives plenty of challenging touches. The main technical theme should relate to the session objectives.

Tactical application

Good coaching is about rehearsing situations that might occur in a game, so that when they do arise the goalkeeper will be able to recognise and deal with them. It is widely acknowledged that goalkeepers are measured by the mistakes they make, so any coaching programme should be concerned with reducing the number of errors. Since mistakes are usually due to a lapse in technique, an incorrect decision or a poor starting position, the coach should organise simulated match situations so that the keeper learns to consistently make the correct response.

Goalkeeping fitness

Given that the session will involve lots of realistic touches of the ball, it should have a beneficial impact on:

- Agility.
- Power/ strength.
- Speed off and across the ground.
- Endurance.

Players start to lose flexibility from ten years of age, so it is very important to include longer stretching work to maintain suppleness. Work on flexibility is recommended when the muscles and connective tissues are warm, either in the middle or at the end of sessions.

Cool-down

A warm-down or cool-down at the end of the session is necessary for the following reasons:

- The body can gradually adjust from an active to resting state.
- The body can rid itself of the waste products of exercise.
- The likelihood of post-exercise muscle soreness is reduced.

Debriefing

A few minutes spent summarising the key factors of a session using a question and answer technique can check the players' understanding, consolidate their learning and reinforce points for future reference.

EVALUATING SESSIONS

The good coach will always honestly evaluate his session to assess whether the objectives were met and to shape his planning for future sessions. Generally speaking the coach should ask himself: Were the players maximally involved? Did they improve? And most importantly: Did they have fun?

The following checklist might prove helpful in evaluating sessions.

- How many opportunities did they have to improve techniques and skills?

- To what extent were the players engaged in the practices and committed to improving their performance?

- How appropriate was the service?

- To what extent did the practices challenge them in a realistic way?

- How well did the players cooperate with each other in the various tasks?

- To what extent were they able to relate the techniques and skills learnt to the game situation?

- What were the signs that the players left the session with increased confidence?

- To what extent did the session improve the players' level of understanding?

- To what degree did the session achieve the intended outcomes?

4

GETTING READY TO PLAY AND TRAIN

Fail to prepare and prepare to fail

One of soccer's great mysteries (and indeed one of its attractions) is that nothing is certain. There is always the chance that the unexpected might happen. This reflects the fact that all teams and their players are fallible and cannot maintain excellent form for every game. If a coach could market the unknown factor that is responsible for a great performance one weekend and a mediocre one the next, he would make a fortune. If the training is basically the same, week in week out, what is it that accounts for this inconsistency? The obvious answers are luck or the quality of the opposition, but the coach is powerless to affect either of these factors.

However, one of the aspects related to consistency that the coach or player can influence is match preparation. Match preparation entails approaching the game with the right mental attitude and in an optimum state of physical readiness. For many goalkeepers this entails following a pre-match routine that, after a time, can almost become a superstition. On occasions, the player may arrive at the ground not feeling 100 per cent healthy or lacking focus, and the pre-match routine can help to dispel any listlessness and sharpen the mind and body. Having reached this desired level of readiness, it is essential that this condition is maintained throughout the match. The keeper should not lose concentration or allow himself to get cold. He should stay 'switched on' at all times.

MENTAL PREPARATION

Mental rehearsal before matches is as important as the physical warm-up. The goalkeeper should visualise previous situations in which he has played well and relive them in his mind. By doing this he will approach the game in a positive manner. This type of mental preparation is useful in restoring confidence after a mistake in a previous game. All negative thoughts should be banished as the goalkeeper imagines himself making an error-free match-winning performance.

Once into the game, no keeper will be too upset by the shot that flies into the top right-hand corner, but he will lose sleep over the one that trickles through his legs. The goalkeeper must aim to eradicate costly mistakes from his game. If a goal is to be conceded, it should be due to brilliance on the part of the opponents, a defensive blunder in front of him or a fluke. When this aim is realised on a regular basis, the reliability of the keeper will be confirmed and confidence will spread throughout the team.

All keepers make mistakes, but the best make the fewest. So how does he avoid letting in too many 'soft' goals? The way in which the keeper approaches a game should not alter because of the quality of the opposition. Time and time again, supposedly superior sides have come unstuck because they underestimated the other team. Thus the goalkeeper should remember to: 'Treat every shot with respect'. By religiously following this motto, concentration on the basics will be enhanced and, in turn, the number of errors will be greatly reduced.

But despite this resolution, the odd mistake will still be made. The way in which the keeper responds after making a mistake is crucial. None of us can change history, so it is important to put mistakes at the back of your mind and get on with the rest of the match. Dwelling on mistakes during the game will affect confidence and concentration. Mistakes can be analysed afterwards and used as a learning experience. After all, we are only human and prone to the odd lapse.

There are three basic types of reaction to making a mistake.

- Confidence crumbles. Due to one mistake, the keeper loses all faith in his ability and the positive attitude with which he began the match evaporates rapidly. Further situations, similar to the one in which the error occurred, fill him with terror. His obvious state of nervousness is recognised both by the opposition, who exploit it, and by his own team, who lose faith in him.

- The goalkeeper tries too hard. In an attempt to atone for his error, the keeper involves himself in situations without assessing them appropriately. Rather than allowing play to develop and dealing with problems in the appropriate manner, he makes rash decisions in order to get to the ball quickly. He feels the need to redeem himself immediately.

- The keeper permits himself only a moment's self-indulgence and gets on with the remainder of the game, determined not to allow the error to affect his confidence or concentration.

For the goalkeeper who has either of the first two reactions above, one mistake can lead to another and eventually to a loss in form. The goalkeeper who can handle set backs, is the one who knows that one mistake does not make a bad player.

PHYSICAL PREPARATION

The warm-up before games may be slightly different to the one before training sessions. This is because the subsequent activity in training is largely controlled by the coach and the warm-up will follow a gradual progression towards the targeted level of work via exercises related to the theme of the session. In a game,

on the other hand, the goalkeeper may be required to perform maximally in the first minute.

The physiological objectives of a pre-match warm-up are:

- To increase the core body temperature by at least one or two degrees.
- To increase the heart rate and subsequently the blood flow to the skeletal tissues
- To increase the activation of the central nervous system in order to heighten coordination, skill accuracy and reaction time.
- To increase the rate and force of muscle contraction
- To increase the suppleness of connective tissue which will reduce the incidences of muscle and tendon injury.

There are four phases to the warm-up:

Phase 1: Aerobic activity
Slow jogging – forwards, backwards and sideways to raise the body temperature and activate the energy production systems.

Phase 2: Dynamic stretches
Dynamic exercises designed to stretch the muscles through their full range of movement. They will involve the shoulders, hips, pelvic area, hamstrings, quadriceps, hip flexors, gluteus muscles, groin and calf. See below for more details.

Phase 3: Movement preparation
Striding out followed by sprinting forwards and backwards in straight lines and zigzag patterns, crossovers, power skips and then specific movements such as jumping.

Phase 4: Ball work
These exercises will involve ball familiarity as well as recreating actions likely to be undertaken during the game. This phase can also familiarise the keeper with the prevailing environmental conditions.

Dynamic Stretches

Arm pumps (for chest, shoulder and upper back)
Work on running form, starting at slow speed then increasing. Maintain a 90° angle at the elbow – 10–15 seconds in each direction.

Hand walks (for calves, hamstrings and glutes)
Start in the press-up position, walk feet up to hands and back out to a press-up position. Repeat three times.

Arm circles (for chest, shoulder and upper back)
Move the arms like a windmill starting in small circles and then increase the range – 10–15 seconds in each direction.

Side bends (for triceps, upper back, abdominals and obliques)
Bend to one side while holding the opposite arm overhead and then quickly change direction and stretch the other side in a continued motion – 10 stretches each side.

Leg swings – front/back/side 15 seconds on each (for calves, hamstrings, hip flexors and glutes)
While holding onto something for balance, move the limb in a controlled manner through the full range. Try to remain upright. Repeat on both legs for 15 seconds.

High knee to chest (for shoulders, glutes, quads and lower back)
While standing, pull one knee to the chest and hold for three seconds. Repeat on other leg.

Trunk twist (for hip flexors, upper back, abdominals and obliques)
With the pelvis kept stationary, twist at the trunk while looking over the shoulder in the direction of the stretch – five stretches each side.

Walking high knees (for shoulders, glutes, quads and lower back)

Take an exaggerated high step bringing up the knee as high as possible while pushing on the toes of the opposite foot at the same time. Use a proper arm swing 90° at the elbow with hands level with the chin on the upswing. Walk over 10 metres.

Walking lunge (for glutes, hamstrings, hip flexors and claves)

Take a long stride striking the heel of the front foot while extending onto the toes of the back foot. Complete the movement by bringing the trailing leg through and standing upright. Place the hands behind the head with the eyes focused forward. Walk over 10 metres.

Walking straight leg kicks (for hamstrings, calves and lower back)

While walking forwards with the front leg straight, kick up the leg and with the fingers of the opposite hand, touch the toes. Repeat on the other leg and walk over 10 metres.

Walking side lunge, over and back (for groin, glutes, hamstrings and ankles)

With the torso upright take a long stride out to the side. Lunge out bending the forward knee to 90° while keeping the trailing leg straight. Lower the legs and shift the body weight to the opposite leg. Finish the movement by bringing the feet together and standing upright. Work over 10 metres.

Running heel flicks (for quads and hip flexors)

With the body leaning forward, run on the balls of the feet while flicking out the heels to touch the buttocks. Work over 10 metres for a minimum of 20 flicks.

Running carioca (for abductors, adductors, glutes, ankles and hips)

Adopting a semi-squat position, take the body weight on the balls of the feet. Twist the hips crossing one leg in front of the other while bringing the trailing leg through and then cross the lead leg behind the trailing leg. The shoulders must remain square throughout the exercise.

Ball familiarity exercises

Select examples from Chapter 5 on ball familiarity in order to focus the mind on the task ahead.

Handling exercises

- Comfortable body shots from 10–12 yards to warm-up the hands.
- The keeper stands on the 6-yard line and the server on the penalty spot. The server throws the ball over the head of the keeper who has to back-pedal in order to make the catch. Five repetitions.
- Concentrated handling. The server throws or volleys the ball from a distance of 8 yards. Twenty repetitions.
- From a distance of 10 yards the server pitches the ball in front of the keeper who has to react smartly to pick it up. Ten repetitions.
- In a 4-yard goal, the server pushes the ball from a distance of 6–8 yards to the side of the goalkeeper who dives to save. Five repetitions on each side.
- From a distance of 12–15 yards the server drives the ball towards the keeper from the angle of the penalty area. Six repetitions from each side of the penalty area.
- The server takes a variety of shots from the edge of the penalty area.
- Fielding crosses from both sides (throw the ball if the service is unreliable). Six crosses from each side. Return the ball to the crosser using a variety of throws and kicks.

Distribution exercises

- The server provides ten passes that the goalkeeper has to control and return without using the hands. The service should be varied to test the keeper's control.
- The keeper executes the three kicking techniques – the drill, wedge and drive – six times.
- The server plays the ball to alternate sides and the keeper has to execute three first-time clearances with his strong and weak foot.

It is important that the goalkeeper is accompanied by another player or coach whose service is reliable so that the keeper begins the game in the best possible physical and mental state. Whether the keeper chooses to use the above exercises or not, it is vital that he acclimatises himself with the ground and weather conditions. Handling practice in the goalmouth will give him some indication of what type of bounce to expect and what influence the sun and wind might have.

The care of equipment

As befits his specialist position, the goalkeeper should possess a range of exclusive accessories. As part of his general preparation it is very important that he keeps his equipment in excellent working order.

Boots

Since one slip can result in a goal conceded, the keeper should regularly check the length of his studs to ensure that they are appropriate for the prevailing ground conditions. In simple terms, short studs for hard surfaces and long studs for muddy surfaces.

Jersey and shorts

It is essential that these two items allow for the full range of movement. A loose-fitting jersey is preferable to one that is just the right size. Shoulder and elbow padding are a matter of personal choice since it is important that the goalkeeper feels comfortable. Such padding can be useful when ground conditions are hard. The wearing of one or two undershirts is advisable on cold days. As with the jersey, shorts should be comfortable and spacious. There is a variety of styles on the market, with or without padding: once again, it is a matter of personal preference.

Goalkeeping trousers

Goalkeeping trousers are recommended for playing on icy grounds or on pitches with bare goalmouths towards the end of the season. The bane of goalkeepers' lives is the frequent friction burns inflicted on the outside of the upper thigh by diving on hard surfaces. Such injuries could be reduced by the wearing of protective shorts or long trousers. Once again, comfort and a full range of movement should determine what is worn. If the keeper prefers not to wear trousers, then petroleum jelly smeared on the knees and thighs may reduce abrasions.

Cap

All goalkeepers should have a cap. It is a difficult skill catching in one hand while shielding the eyes from the sun with the other! The

keeper should ensure that the peak is large enough and that the cap does not fall off the head too easily.

Gloves

Although goalkeeping gloves can considerably increase the effectiveness of handling, the keeper must not forget that it is the hands inside them that are important. Even though most gloves give an excellent grip, fingers and thumbs should still be spread well to the side and behind the ball if the catch is to be 100 per cent safe.

Gloves will last longer and provide a better grip if they are well maintained.

There are three steps to glove care.

1 Always wash gloves immediately after matches or training in water not exceeding 86°F (30°C). A sponge will clean off surface dirt without causing abrasions to the latex palm. Do not use detergents.

2 After rinsing carefully with clean water, allow the gloves to drip-dry away from direct heat or sunlight.

3 Dampening the latex palm before games will improve handling. When playing in wet or muddy conditions it is recommended that the keeper takes a rag or sponge out on to the field of play so that dirt can be removed from the palm when necessary.

It is sensible to keep the newest pair of gloves for matches and to use the more worn ones for training. It is recommended that new pairs of gloves are 'broken in' and worn prior to the game. If conditions are particularly wet or muddy, it is advisable to use old gloves for the warm-up and to save the best pair for the match.

BALL FAMILIARITY

5

The ball is the enemy, but the goalkeeper should make it his friend

If players are to fulfil their potential it is essential that they are comfortable with the ball. For the goalkeeper this entails good ball control with feet as well as with the hands. As mentioned previously, every session should incorporate practices designed to improve the goalkeeper's ability to play the ball with his feet. Involving the keeper in outfield exercises such as 'keep ball' will do wonders for his control and passing skills.

As far as handling is concerned, the goalkeeper must be able to control the ball with consummate ease. By constantly flipping the ball back and forth using all parts of the hand, wrist and lower arm, the keeper will soon develop this 'friendship' with the ball. In the modern game, shots often swerve and dip, so the goalkeeper should be prepared to improvise and present a barrier to keep the ball out. The more familiar he is with the ball, the less likely he is to be caught off guard by a sudden deviation in its flight.

This chapter will provide a number of individual exercises geared to helping the goalkeeper to be more comfortable with the ball. The list is by no means exhaustive; the exercises should be as broad as the goalkeeper's or coach's imagination. It is recommended that every warm-up for either matches or training incorporates ball familiarity exercises.

BALL FAMILIARITY EXERCISES

(1) Keep the ball in the air using palms, backs of hands, wrists and forearms. Try to use a different surface on each contact. Count the number of continuous contacts before the ball hits the ground. Try to beat previous record. (See photos 1a and 1b.)

(2) Using the fingers of both hands, flip the ball continuously above the head. Withdraw the fingers slightly on each contact so that the ball is kept under control. (See photo 2.)

Photo 1a and b Keepy uppy with the hands, wrists and forearms

(3) As in (2), but this time using the fists. Progress from one hand only to both in a left-right, left-right combination. The ball should only be played 12–24 inches above head level. Again, try to beat your previous record. Having mastered this practice, try to set more difficult challenges such as going down to a kneeling and even lying position without breaking the sequence. (See photo 3.) When punching, it is important to remember the following points.

- Present a flat surface with the knuckles – do not close the fist too tightly.
- Keep the wrist stiff.
- Keep the ball in front at eye level.

Photo 2 Finger flipping   Photo 3 Punching

(4) Transfer the ball from one hand to the other, passing it around the body.

(5) As in (4), but this time pass the ball in a figure of eight manner around and through the legs. Then try a combination of round the body and through the legs. (See photos 4a and 4b.)

Photo 4a and 4b Figure of eight handling

(6) Hold the ball with one hand in front of the legs and the other behind. Quickly switch the position of the hands without the ball hitting the ground. (See photo 5.)

Photo 5 Switching hands

(7) Hold the ball with both hands in front of the legs. Quickly switch so that the hands move behind the legs and catch the ball before it hits the ground. (See photo 6.)

Photo 6 Swapping hands

(8) Hold the ball in the right hand as high and as far away from the body as possible. In a continuous motion, sweep the ball down in front of the body, taking it in the left hand to the highest and furthest point from the body. Continue in this manner, ensuring a smooth transfer from one hand to the other.

(9) Keeping both feet pointing forwards, hold the ball in the right hand, level with the shoulder. Twist the trunk so that the ball is taken to the furthest point behind the body. Repeat with the left hand. (See photos 7a and 7b.)

Photo 7a and 7b Trunk twists

Photo 8 Half-volley pick-ups

(10) Holding the ball out to the side of the body with the right hand, drop it and catch it again on the half-volley. Try to do this at full stretch, ensuring that the ball is caught just after it hits the ground. Repeat with the left hand. (See photo 8.)

(11) As in (10), but this time moving and picking up the ball on the half-volley.

(12) Flip the ball over the shoulder using the right hand. Back pedal quickly and arch the back to catch the ball in the left hand. (See photo 9.)

Photo 9 Flipping ball over shoulder

(13) Moving about the goal area, bounce the ball and catch it, checking that the fingers and thumbs form a 'W' shape. Progress to bouncing the ball like a basketball player. This is a particularly good exercise to perform before matches to enable the goalkeeper to familiarise himself with the ground conditions.

(14) Throw or kick the ball into the air and jump to catch the ball at arms length. Ensure that the ball is caught at the highest safest point in front at eye level, with slightly bent arms and with the 'W' grip. This exercise will help the goalkeeper acclimatise to any problems caused by the sun or wind.

(15) Roll the ball along the ground and sprint to pick it up. In order to pick up the ball without slowing down, ensure that the leading foot is placed alongside the ball and that the hands scoop up the ball in one fluid motion. (See photo 10.)

Photo 10 Roll and pick up

(16) Holding the ball in the hands, perform a forward roll without losing possession.

(17) Throw the ball into the air and trap it as it hits the ground. Roll out of the save so that the original standing position is regained in one smooth movement. To execute a safe trap, the first hand goes round the ball and the second on top. (See photo 11.)

Photo 11 Dive and trap

(18) Tap the ball from one foot to the other. Progress to a hop between each contact.

(19) Lightly touch the top of the ball with the sole of the foot Alternate the feet rapidly. (See photo 12.)

Photo 12 Toe tapping

(20) As in (19), but push the ball forwards for ten paces and then drag it backwards to the original starting position.

(21) Drop the ball to execute a wedge trap using the inside of the right foot. Repeat the movement using the outside of the right foot. Then follow the same procedure using the left foot. (See photos 13a and 13b.)

Photo 13a and 13b Wedge control

(22) Throw the ball over the head and spin around to control it using one of the techniques described in (21).

Look after the basics and the great saves will take care of themselves

The majority of goalkeeping mistakes are attributable to a lapse in basic technique, so it is absolutely essential that the keeper regularly practises the fundamentals. Mastery of the basics will result in the goalkeeper making the difficult look easy and, more importantly, help to reduce the number of mistakes.

There is nothing more galling than to hear coaches or players console a keeper who has just made a glaring error by saying 'unlucky'. 'Unlucky' should refer to a deflection or some other kind of fluke and not to a lack of application of the basics. There are three fundamental areas that require constant attention.

HEAD

The head should be rock steady so that the eyes are on the ball at all times. At no point should the keeper turn his head away when making a save. It is crucial to take the ball in front of the eye-line so that it can always be seen.

HANDS

The keeper lives or dies on the strength of his handling. Good handling is the equivalent of an outfield player's 'touch', so the goalkeeper must constantly strive to perfect this all-important technique.

Frequent polishing of handling skills in training will enhance the goalkeeper's self-esteem and result in him approaching the next match in a positive frame of mind. When conditions are dry, occasionally undertaking handling practice without gloves can improve the keeper's feel of the ball by making him concentrate on the correct placement of fingers and thumbs. Also, catching cleanly without the assistance of gloves can do wonders for confidence.

FEET

Good footwork can make a difficult save look easy. Diving often involves a risk because for some time there is no barrier behind the hands. Moving quickly in to line with the ball, so that some part of the body is behind the hands, will ensure that there is 'double cover'.

When preparing to receive a shot the legs should be a shoulder width apart, knees slightly bent, head steady, shoulders ahead of the feet and the weight on the toes. This is the 'ready' or 'set' position (see photo 14). If the legs are too wide apart, it is difficult to move quickly or achieve good spring and, of course, the ball might pass through them.

Photo 14 The ready position

Whenever possible, body weight should be tipping forwards so that if the ball is mishandled a second save can be made almost immediately. If the ball is half-saved and the keeper falls backwards, it takes longer to recover and by that time it is usually too late.

The majority of practices in this chapter are designed for either individual or pair work, and will prove useful in training situations where space and suitable facilities are at a premium. If the quality of practice is to be sustained, however, it is vital that the service is reliable and, with young players, the coach would be well advised to spend some time perfecting feeding techniques.

FOOTWORK EXERCISES

(1) Running over balls/markers

Organisation

Six to eight balls are laid out in a line with a ball's space in between them. The goalkeeper has to run over the balls, placing a foot in each space. (See photo 15.)

Key points

- Light, quick steps.
- Keep weight on the balls of the feet.

Photo 15 Running over balls

(2) Gliding round balls/markers

Organisation

Six to eight balls are laid out as in (1), but this time the goalkeeper glides sideways, in and out of the balls. (See photo 16.)

Photo 16 Gliding round balls

Key points

- Glide with feet a shoulder-width apart and knees bent.
- Try to keep feet in contact with the ground as much as possible.
- Keep the body weight forward with the shoulders ahead of the feet.

(3) Gliding in and out of balls/markers

Organisation

As in (2), but this time the goalkeeper approaches the balls/markers front on. (See photo 17.)

Photo 17 Gliding in and out of balls front on

Key points

- Move forwards and backwards with both feet in line and a shoulder-width apart.
- Try to keep feet in contact with the ground as much as possible.
- Keep the body weight forward with the shoulders ahead of the feet.

(4) Gliding around one ball

Organisation

The keeper glides around one ball in a clockwise motion. After three circuits, repeat in an anticlockwise motion. (See photo 18.)

Key points

As in (3) above.

Photo 18 Gliding round one ball

Photo 19 Bunny hopping   **Photo 20** Side stepping

(5) Zigzagging around balls/markers

Organisation

The balls/markers are arranged in a zigzag formation and the goalkeeper has to glide around each ball/marker. Progress to moving backwards in and out of the balls/markers. To test whether the keeper is moving with the head up, the coach can feed in the occasional ball so that the keeper has to save on the move.

Key points

- Glide with feet a shoulder-width apart and knees bent.
- Maintain good contact with the ground.
- Keep body weight forward.
- Try to move in the ready position with head up and hands cocked.

(6) Other variations

Using his imagination, the coach can devise a number of other footwork exercises that could add variety to the session. For example, side-stepping, hopping or bunny-jumping over the balls. (See photos 19 and 20.)

(7) One-handed glides

Organisation

Standing two paces away from the keeper, the server feeds the ball to alternate sides. The keeper has to glide and catch the ball with one hand and return it to the server. As the practice develops the server can work with two balls to increase the intensity of the exercise.

Key points

- Glide with feet a shoulder-width apart, knees bent and body weight forward.
- Move on the balls of the feet.
- Try to move in line with the ball as much as possible.
- When moving backwards, use small, mincing steps.

All the aforementioned practices are not only important in their own right but are also excellent warm-up exercises.

(8) The square

Organisation

The keeper stands in 3-yard × 3-yard square while the coach, standing 2 yards away, throws the ball at a variety of heights. The coach mixes the service so that some balls are played low to the front of the square while others are played high to the back. The keeper has to move his feet quickly and catch all balls with two hands. The coach can increase the intensity and the degree of difficulty depending on the needs of the keeper.

Key points

- Move lightly and quickly on the balls of the feet.
- Use small steps to get close to the ball.
- Keep the ball in view at all times.
- Catch the ball with two hands.

HANDLING EXERCISES

(1) One-handed catches – five lives

Learning to catch the ball with one hand has the benefit of teaching the goalkeeper how to develop 'soft' hands by taking the pace off the ball (using the arms as shock absorbers). It also gives the goalkeeper tremendous confidence in his handling.

Organisation

In pairs, standing at a distance of 5–10 yards, throw the ball at varying heights and speeds to each other. Start with five points or lives and every time the ball is dropped or caught with two hands a life is lost. Once five lives are lost the game is over. Introducing competition will increase levels of concentration.

Key points
- Move into line.
- Keep the head steady.
- Withdraw the arm slightly on contact to take the pace off the ball ('soft hands').

(2) Two ball, one-handed catches

Organisation

In pairs, standing 5 yards apart and using two balls, the keeper throws left handed to his partner's right hand while simultaneously catching the other ball with his right hand.

Key points

As (1) above

(3) Two ball game

Organisation

The goalkeeper, holding a ball, faces the server who stands 2 yards away. As the server throws the ball (no. 1) to the keeper's right-hand side, the keeper throws his ball (no. 2) back to the server and glides to catch ball no. 1. The server then throws ball no. 2 to the left of the keeper, who at the same moment returns ball no. 1 to the server. The process is repeated until the intended number of serves is reached. The practice requires good coordination between keeper and server. Twenty serves will be sufficient for younger keepers. (See photo 21).

Key points
- Glide into line, keeping the feet a shoulder width apart.
- Keep the head steady.
- Quick hands.

Photo 21 Two ball game

CATCHING TECHNIQUES

The four hand shapes

There are four basic hand shapes when catching the ball, the first three are used for shots straight at the keeper and the fourth for ground shots away from the keeper:

- The scoop – both hands behind the ball for ground shots straight at the keeper (see photo 22).

Photo 22 The scoop

- The cup – trapping the ball into the midriff for the waist height shots straight at the keeper (see photo 23).

Photo 23 The Cup

- 'W' and shock absorber – fingers and thumbs spread to the side and behind the ball (forming a 'W' shape) for shots at upper chest height and above. The forearms should be used as shock absorbers to take the pace off the ball (see photo 24a and 24b).

Photo 24a and 24b 'W' and shock absorbers

- Hands leading – first hand behind to stop the ball and second hand on top to trap it for those ground shots away from the keeper. This is commonly known as the collapsing save where the keeper aims for soft landings so that the impact of hitting the ground is absorbed by the shoulder and side (see photo 25).

Photo 25 Hands leading

(4) The scoop from a kneeling position

Organisation

The goalkeeper kneels, and with the server three or four paces away, the ball is kicked along the ground straight at the keeper. The coach starts with two touch service but progresses to one touch. (See photo 22.)

Key points

- With elbows slightly bent, open the palms to face the ball with fingers spread.
- Position the hands together behind the ball.
- Allow the ball to roll into the hands before cradling into the body.
- Keep the head steady with eyes fixed on the ball.

(5) The scoop from a standing position – choosing the barrier

Organisation

The keeper defends a goal 2 yards wide. The ball is played along the ground towards the keeper's feet from a distance of 6–10 yards at varying speeds. There are four basic methods that can be used when dealing with this type of shot, and the goalkeeper must use the one he feels is most appropriate at the time. Each of them is designed to provide a second barrier behind the hands. One effective way of perfecting the various barriers is to stop the ball without using the hands.

Key points for the long barrier method

- Adopt the ready position.
- Move into line with the ball
- Bend one knee forwards and turn the other leg sideways so that a long barrier is formed.
- With both hands behind the ball, scoop it safely into the chest. (See photo 26.)

Photo 26 Long barrier

Key points for the bending from the hips method

- Adopt the ready position.
- Move into line with the ball.
- Move the legs to less than the width of a ball.
- With both hands behind the ball, scoop it safely into the chest. (See photo 27.)

Photo 27 Bending from the hips

Key points for the 'K' method

- Adopt the ready position.
- Move into line with the ball.
- Bend one knee forwards and turn the other leg sideways so that a 'K' shape is formed.
- With both hands behind the ball, scoop it safely into the chest. (See photo 28.)

Photo 28 The K

Key points for the collapsing forward method recommended for those shots delivered with extra pace or slightly off-centre

- Adopt the ready position.
- Move into the flight of the ball to scoop the ball. As the ball enters the hands, collapse the legs towards the ground.

It is important that the goalkeeper masters the aforementioned techniques so that he can choose the most appropriate (and crucially the safest) method. (See photos 29a, 29b and 29c.)

Photo 29 a/b/c Collapsing scoop

(6) The cup from a kneeling position

Organisation

The goalkeeper kneels, and with the server three or four paces away, the ball is kicked or thrown to the keeper's midriff. The coach starts with two-touch service but progresses to one-touch.

Key points
- With elbows bent and tucked in, palms face upwards with fingers spread.
- Cup the ball into the body.
- Keep the head steady with eyes fixed on the ball. (See photo 23.)

(7) The cup from a standing position – volleyed service

Organisation

The keeper defends a goal 2 yards wide. The ball is volleyed, played towards the keeper's midriff from a distance of four to six paces at varying speeds. Work in sets of 10/20/30. Keep a record of the number of fumbles so that the score can be improved on the next attempt.

Key points
- Adopt the ready position with head steady, feet a shoulder-width apart, knees slightly bent, weight on the balls of the feet, hands ready (as if wearing handcuffs).
- Move into line with the ball.
- For balls delivered between the waist and chest use the cup hand shape.
- Keep the head steady with eyes fixed on the ball.
- Stand firm – do not step backwards.

(8) The cup – pick-ups

Organisation

The keeper defends a goal 2 yards wide. With the server 6–10 yards away, the ball is thrown or volleyed so that it pitches in front of the keeper at varying speeds and lengths. Work in sets of 10/20/30. Keep a record of the number of fumbles so that the score can be improved on the next attempt.

Key points
- Adopt the ready position with head steady, feet a shoulder-width apart, knees slightly bent, weight on the balls of the feet, hands ready (as if wearing handcuffs).
- Move into line with the ball.
- Assess the pace and bounce of the ball.
- Use the cup hand shape to secure the ball.

- Keep the head steady with eyes fixed on the ball.
- If there is a lot of pace on the ball, collapse forward and go to ground (see photos 29a, 29b, 29c).

(9) **Ws and shock absorbers from a sitting position**

Organisation

The goalkeeper sits on the ground with the server standing three to six paces away. The server either throws or volleys towards the goalkeeper's upper chest and head. (See photo 30.)

Photo 30 Ws from a sitting position

Key points

- Keep the head steady with the eyes fixed on the ball.
- Use the forearms as shock absorbers to take the pace off the ball.
- Spread the fingers and thumbs to the side of and behind the ball to form a 'W' shape.
- Flick the ball back to the server to strengthen the fingers.

(10) **Ws and shock absorbers from a standing position**

Organisation

The ball is thrown or volleyed towards the keeper's body from a distance of 6–8 yards. Work in sets of 10/20/30. Keep a record of the number of fumbles so that the score can be beaten on the next attempt.

Key points

- Adopt the ready position with head steady, feet a shoulder-width apart, knees slightly bent, weight on the balls of the feet, hands ready (as if wearing handcuffs).
- Move into line with the ball.
- For shots chest height and above, use shock absorbers and 'Ws'.
- Stand firm – do not step backwards.

(11) **Selecting the correct hand shape and barrier**

Having mastered the correct hand shapes for balls played straight at the keeper in isolated practices, it is important to test the keeper's decision making with a variety of service.

Organisation

Defending a 2-yard goal the keeper deals with a variety of shots delivered from a distance of 6–10 yards. The keeper should face some balls played along the ground, some pitched in front of him and some through the air.

Key points

- Adopt the ready position.
- Assess the pace and flight of the ball.
- Glide into line.
- Use the appropriate hand shape and barrier.

(12) **1 v 1 throwing to score**

Organisation

Working in pairs using two small goals (2 yards wide) over a distance of 10–15 yards, the goalkeeper has to beat his partner with a throw. Progress to a kicked service. (See photo 31.)

Photo 31 Throwing to score

Key points

- Adopt the ready position.
- Assess the pace and flight of the ball.
- Glide into line.
- Use the appropriate hand shape and barrier.

(13) Catching away from the body

Organisation

In pairs the keepers stands 10–20 yards apart and provide a variety of thrown and kicked services. They have to catch the ball without trapping it into the body. This forces them to move their feet in order to get into position to catch away from the body.

Key points

- Glide into line quickly.
- Keep the head steady.
- Select the appropriate hand shape.

This practice is excellent for developing fast footwork combined with confident handling.

(14) Catching and pulling balls into the body

Organisation

As in (13) above, but without the restriction of catching away from the body.

Key points

As in (13) above.

DIVING TECHNIQUES

For the youngster, diving is the most exciting aspect of goalkeeping. However, as in all sports, skilled performance is about making the difficult look easy and the keeper must not dive just to be spectacular. The keeper only dives when he has insufficient time to move the feet to get into line with the shot. In effect, it is an emergency action in the same way that a sliding tackle is. Many youngsters have a side on which they prefer to dive but the coach, by stripping the technique down, can diagnose the cause of this preference and rectify the weakness.

(1) The collapsing save

One of the most difficult saves that a keeper is faced with is the shot which passes quickly by his feet. His legs have to collapse away and he must lead with his hands because they can drop on the ball before the body can. This save involves the fourth hand shape – hands leading – and as it is a complicated technique, it is advisable to introduce it with the keeper on his knees before progressing to his haunches, then crouching and finally standing. Starting the first practice on the knees means that attention can be focused on reaching for the ball early so that the hand shape is correct and that the landing impact is taken on the shoulders.

Organisation

The goalkeeper kneels in a goal 4–5 yards in length. The server stands 6–8 yards away and passes the ball to one side of the keeper. Having made the save, the ball is returned to the server, who takes a touch before passing to the other side. Once the correct hand shape and landing have been achieved, progress to the keeper on his haunches, then crouching and finally standing. The keeper must be allowed to recover and return to the ready position between saves. Progress to varied and close range service. (See photos 32a and 32b.)

Photo 32a and 32b The collapsing save

Key points

- Adopt the ready position (when standing).
- React to the ball (do not go down too early).
- Collapse the legs.
- Lead with both hands in front of the line of the body so that the dive is slightly forward.
- Place the first hand behind the ball to stop it, the second hand on top of the ball to trap it.
- Soft landings (on side and shoulder).
- Pull the ball into the body.

One of the most common faults, particularly in young keepers, is the tendency to land on the elbow which causes the ball to be fumbled. By extending the arms out in front of the body, the goalkeeper will take the impact of the dive on the shoulder rather than the elbow. Another common mistake is the keeper rotating on to his back on landing. Here the focus should be on taking the landing impact on the shoulder rather than the upper back. Generally speaking if the goalkeeper is experiencing a problem go back a stage to crouching or even kneeling so that he can execute the technique successfully. Learning the correct technique at an early age can prevent the development of bad habits, so the coach should be patient and persevere.

(2) Low diving save

Organisation

The goalkeeper sits on his haunches. After bouncing the ball as a signal of his intention to throw, the server, standing 3 yards away, feeds the ball to the side of the keeper, who springs to catch the ball. Six repetitions on each side. Progress to crouching and then full standing position. (See photos 33a to 33c.)

Key points

- Adopt the ready position (when standing).
- Lead with the hands as if wearing handcuffs.
- Step into the line of the ball with the nearest foot.
- Push hard off near the leg.
- Shock absorber 'Ws' handling method.
- Soft landings on shoulder and side (not the elbows).

The coach should look for common faults, such as landing on the elbows, rotating, or diving flat so the keeper ends up on his front. Once again the remedy is usually found by identifying the problem and going back to one of the more basic exercises to build up confidence.

(3) The glory save

Organisation

The goalkeeper starts in the middle of the goal. The server stands level with the post 6 yards from the goal line. After bouncing the ball as a signal of his intention to throw, the server feeds the ball just inside the post. The goalkeeper has to spring to save. The service increases in difficulty as the keeper progresses so that he may have to use one or two glide movements before taking off. (See photo 34.)

Key points

- Adopt the ready position.
- Step into the line of the ball with the nearest foot.
- Good spring
- Shock absorber 'Ws' hand shape.
- Soft landings.

Photo 33a, 33b and 33c The low diving save

Photo 34 The glory save

PART II
THE FIVE
GOALKEEPING ROLES

SHOT STOPPING
CATCHING, DEFLECTING AND PARRYING

7

Good goalkeepers make the difficult saves look easy

Having mastered the basics, the keeper should approach shot-stopping with increased confidence. The good coach will ensure that training sessions involve shots at varying heights, speeds and angles in order to recreate situations that the keeper might face during a match. This will entail dealing with shots delivered along and off the ground as well as balls played through the air.

Throughout the practices the keeper should strive for perfection but he should realise that sometimes a save will be incomplete. While catching the ball is the preferred outcome there will be times when this is not possible. On those occasions he should at least control where the ball goes and be ready to make an immediate second save. He must not relax until the danger has been effectively nullified.

(1) Dual

Organisation
Two goalkeepers face each other 15–20 yards apart, each defending a small goal (6 yards wide) using markers. The object is for each goalkeeper to score with a kick from the ground.

Key points
- Get into line
- Be 'set' as the shot is struck.
- Assess the flight and pace on the ball.
- Use the appropriate saving technique.
- React quickly to make any second saves if necessary.

(2) Bouncers and skimmers in and around the body

Organisation
The server, from a distance of 15–18 yards, fires shots in and around the goalkeeper. A marker placed 1 yard inside each post will provide a useful guide for the service which should include half-volleys which skim across the surface and volleys that pitch in front of the keeper.

Key points
- Get into line.
- Be 'set' as the shot is struck.
- Assess the flight, bounce and pace on the ball.
- Use the appropriate saving technique.
- React quickly to make a second saves if necessary.

(3) Deflecting the ball round the post/ to safety

Organisation
This practice takes place in a 6-yard goal with a safety zone marked each side of the post two feet from the goal line (see Figure 1). It is designed to help the keeper make the correct split-second decision as to whether to catch the ball or deflect it to safety. The decision is based entirely on the degree of difficulty, which is determined by the placement and the pace on the shot. The server stands 8 yards from the goal and plays a fast ball just inside the post. The keeper has to decide whether to execute a collapsing save, low diving save or deflect into the safety zone.

Key points
- Adopt the ready position.
- Assess the pace and angle of the shot.
- If catchable, use the appropriate hand shape.
- If deflecting, angle the bottom hand ('a gate not a plate') to divert the ball to safety.
- Rise quickly, ready for a second save if necessary.

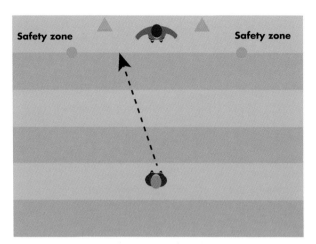

Figure 1 Deflecting the ball to safety

(4) Top hand saves

Often when saving shots bound for the top corners, the keeper has to make a save with the top hand (the hand furthest away from the ball) as this affords the goalkeeper greater reach.

Organisation

The goalkeeper sits on the ground with the server 2-3 yards away. The server throws the ball to the keeper's left side and he reaches across using the right hand only to deflect the ball, which is caught by a second server positioned to the side of the goal. Repeat for the other side. (See photo 35.) Progress to the keeper rising up from the ground before deflecting the ball.

Photo 35 Top hand saves

Key points
• Keep the head steady.
• Reach across the body with the top hand.
• Use the fingers to divert the ball upwards and to the side.

(5) Turning the ball over the bar

Organisation

The keeper stands on the 6-yard line with the server positioned on the penalty spot. The server feeds the ball over the keeper's head, and the keeper has to back-pedal to catch or turn the ball to safety. (See photo 36.)

Photo 36 Turning the ball over the bar

Key points
• Adopt the ready position.
• Take small, mincing steps backwards.
• Take off on one foot.
• If the ball cannot be caught, deflect it over the bar using the fingers.

Deflecting the ball

The aerodynamics of the modern football means that it is not always possible, or safe, to catch so it is important that the keeper masters deflecting and parrying techniques. This entails clever use of the hands with an understanding on how the hand should be angled and what part should be used. In the same way that the tennis player manipulates the racquet head to place the ball in a certain direction, the keeper, through dexterous use of the hands can control where the ball ends up. In looking at what part of the hand should be used it is recommended that the keeper does not use the fist to turn shots over the crossbar or round the post as it is uneven and does not present a reliable controlling surface. However, using the fingers and palm provides a larger surface area, greater sensitivity and reach.

If a shot is not going to be held, the ball should be deflected for a corner or, at worst, outside the line of the posts. In the majority of cases, two hands are better than one since they present a larger barrier. However, there will be occasions when leading with one hand affords extra reach or provides the quickest reaction.

There is a subtle difference between parrying and deflecting the ball.

Parrying the ball is recommended when the pace on the shot is so great that the keeper is not only unable to catch the ball cleanly, but also has difficulty in accurately diverting it. Pushing the ball tamely back into play can present opponents with a second chance. Instead the goalkeeper should use the heels of both hands so that the ball rebounds so fiercely that it travels a good distance and is not easily controlled by the opposition. (See photo 37.)

Deflecting the ball is the best option for those well-directed shots which are difficult to catch. Here the goalkeeper angles the hand or hands (like a half-open gate) and makes contact with the fingers or hand so that the ball is diverted out of play. With practice, the keeper will learn the correct amount of resistance to be allowed by the hand. (See photo 38.) Sometimes his touch can be too strong and the ball comes back into play; on other occasions he will flick the wrist too much and merely help the ball into the net. It is important that, having assessed the difficulty on the shot, the keeper does not get caught in two minds and tries to catch when deflecting is the safest option. This can result in the ball being pushed back into a dangerous area rather than to safety.

Photo 37 Parrying the ball

Photo 38 Deflecting the ball

(6) Catch or parry

Organisation

This practice is designed to help the keeper make the correct split-second decision as to whether to catch the ball or parry it to safety. The decision is based on the degree of difficulty determined by the movement and the pace of the shot. The server stands 10 yards from the goal and volleys the ball towards the middle of the goal with varying degrees of pace. The keeper has to decide whether to catch or parry.

Key points

- Adopt the ready position.
- Stay big for as long as possible.
- Assess the pace and height of the ball.
- Decide whether to catch or parry.
- If parrying use the heels of the hands to rebound the ball as fiercely, and as far away, as possible.
- React quickly to make any secondary saves.

(7) The soft parry

For those shots fired straight at the keeper's upper body that are too hot to handle he can break down the save by executing the soft parry. In this save the goalkeeper uses the W hand shape but instead of catching the ball he slightly withdraws his hands on contact to take the pace off it and pats it down into the ground using soft hands (see photo 39a, 39b and 39c)

Organisation

From a distance of 8 yards the coach volleys the ball hard towards the goalkeeper's upper chest. The keeper takes the pace off the ball by using the soft parry technique. Work in sets of ten before progressing to varying the pace of the ball so that the keeper has to decide whether to catch or execute the soft parry.

Key points

- Adopt the ready position.
- Move into line with the ball.
- Using 'W' hand shape and soft hands pat the ball into the ground.
- Gather the ball on the first bounce.

(8) Off the cones and shoot

Organisation

Two heavyweight cones are bunched together on the edge of the penalty area. The server throws the ball at the cones and fires in the rebound. The keeper makes the save. Occasionally the ball may squeeze through the cones and the keeper must be ready to advance quickly to gather it. Using the cones as a rebounding surface leads to unpredictable shooting angles and therefore keeps the goalkeeper on his toes.

Photo 39a, 39b and 39c The soft parry

Key points

- Adopt a good starting position.
- Get into line quickly.
- Keep the head steady.
- Be 'set' in the ready position as the ball is struck.
- Use the appropriate saving technique.
- React quickly to make any second saves.

(9) 2 v 2

Organisation

Having mastered catching, deflecting and parrying techniques, the goalkeeper is ready to face a variety of shots and demonstrate good decision making and the application of the appropriate saving technique. On a pitch measuring 20 yards in length, there are two goalkeepers in each goal. The object is to score in the opponents' goal using a throw, shot or volley. Each team may have an outfield player to capitalise on rebounds. This is a tremendously demanding and enjoyable practice in which the keepers must be competitive.

(10) Quick-fire shots game

Organisation

This involves one goal and one keeper, with two teams of three players. The pitch is defined by the lines of the penalty area. The coach feeds in balls from the outside and players of both teams are encouraged to shoot at the earliest opportunity. (See Figure 2.)

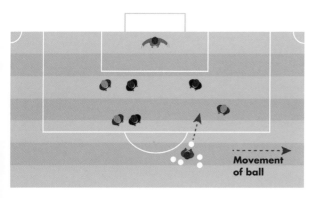

Figure 2 Quick-fire shots game

(11) Small-sided game instant shooting 2 v 2

Organisation

This is a 2 v 2 small-sided game plus two keepers in an area measuring 20 × 20 yards. In this situation the players are encouraged to shoot at the earliest opportunity. Spare players stand either side of each post and can be used as a rebound 'wall' for the outfield players. The team that scores is rewarded with the next possession. (See Figure 3.)

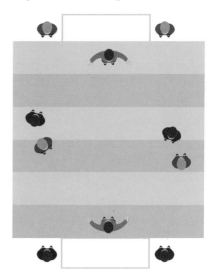

Figure 3 Instant shooting 2 v 2

Key points for (9), (10) and (11)

- Adopt the ready position.
- Get into line quickly.
- Keep the head steady.
- Use the appropriate saving technique.
- React quickly to make any second saves.

SHOT STOPPING
POSITIONING

8

Successful goalkeeping is about being in the right place at the right time

The goalkeeper who masters the art of positioning will make the job look easy. There are two basic movements involved in positioning: (1) moving into line with the ball; (2) moving up the line towards the ball. Linking these two movements is often known as 'narrowing the angle' and the purpose is to reduce the size of the target for the shooter. (See photos 40a and 40b.) The angle and distance of the ball in relation to the goal will determine the keeper's position. The keeper basically works in an arc where the size of the angle is proportional to the distance the goalkeeper has to come down the line. (See Figure 4.) In other words, if the opponent's shooting angle is tight, there is less need to narrow the angle. The whole point of positioning is to reduce the amount of goal shown to the shooter so if he is in a wide position his view of the goal is already diminished.

The experienced keeper will narrow the angle quickly by cutting the diagonal, gliding into line and up the line in one movement. (See Figure 5.)

Photo 40a and 40b Narrowing the angle

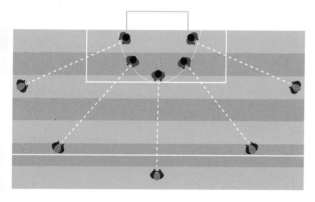

Figure 4 Positioning arc

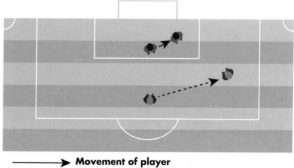

⟶ **Movement of player**
----⟶ **Movement of ball**

Figure 5 Cutting the diagonal

The keeper should be constantly adjusting his position according to where the ball is. Even when play is in the opponents' half, he should be in line with the ball and on the edge of his penalty area, ready to make a timely interception if the ball is played over the defence.

When the ball is in and around the penalty area it is important not to come too far down the line while the ball-carrier still has his head up. The skilled player will chip a keeper who commits himself in this way. It is safer to take the final steps forwards as the ball-carrier is preparing to shoot and has his eyes fixed on the ball.

Finally, it is imperative that the keeper is 'set' in the ready position as the shot is struck, because it is difficult to dive sideways while still moving forwards.

(1) Handball

Organisation
The goalkeeper takes up a position in the middle of the goal. Four servers are stationed around the penalty area. They throw the ball to each other and the keeper has to take up an appropriate position. After each catch, the server should pause so that the coach can assess the keeper's position. Progress to the servers occasionally volleying the ball towards the goal. (See Figure 6.)

Key points
- Get into line – where possible glide in the ready position.
- Get up the line – where possible glide in the ready position.
- Be 'set' in the ready position as the shot is struck.
- Use the appropriate saving technique.
- React quickly to make any second saves.

(2) Angled shots – numbers

Organisation
The coach marks off the goalmouth in sectors (see Figure 7) which are then numbered one to five. A server with a ball is stationed in each sector. On the coach's command one of the servers plays the ball out of his feet and shoots for goal. The goalkeeper reacts to the command by getting into position as quickly as possible.

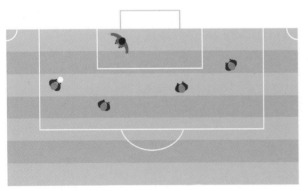

Figure 6 Handball

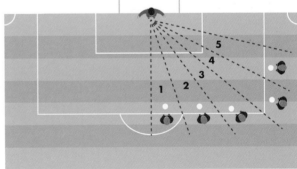

Figure 7 Angle shots – numbers

Key points

- Always expect a shot.
- Cut the diagonal (into line and up the line).
- Glide in the ready position if time permits.
- Be 'set' in the ready position as the ball is struck.
- Use the appropriate saving technique.
- React quickly to make any second saves.

(3) Shooting gallery

Organisation

The coach stands behind the goalkeeper who is faced by a number of servers spread around the edge of the penalty area, each with a ball. The coach points to one server who plays the ball out of his feet and shoots for goal. The keeper has to react quickly to get into line. (See Figure 8.)

Key points

- Pick up the line of the ball quickly.
- Cut the diagonal (into line and up the line).
- Steal an extra step forwards as the shooter addresses the ball.
- Be 'set' in the ready position as the ball is struck.
- Use the appropriate saving technique.
- React quickly to make any second saves.

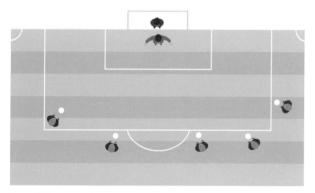

Figure 8 Shooting gallery

(4) Turn and save

Organisation

For this practice the server changes position after every shot and always shoots on the move. The keeper faces the goal and turns on the command. The server waits for the keeper to pick up the line of the ball before shooting.

Key points

- Adopt a good starting position relative to the ball, usually 3–4 yards off the goal line.
- Pick up the line of the ball quickly.
- Cut the diagonal.
- Be 'set' in the ready position as the ball is struck.
- Use the appropriate saving technique.
- React quickly to make any second saves.

(5) Gates

Organisation

Four 1-yard gates (marked with discs), at a various angles, are laid out around the penalty area (See Figure 9). The server plays the ball through the gates and then strikes for goal. The gates should be placed so that the striker shoots with the ball sometimes moving towards and at other times away from the goal in order to create realism.

Key points

As in (4) above.

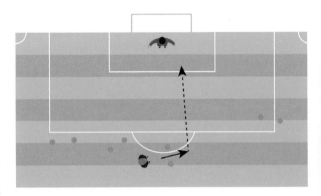

Figure 9 Gates

(6) The fan

Organisation

In this practice four servers stand in a fan formation 15–18 yards from the goal either in central or wide positions. One of the servers on the outside passes the ball into the central player who either lays it off to one of his colleagues or turns to shoot himself. The keeper has to respond in the appropriate manner. (See Figure 10.)

Key points

As in (4) above.

(7) 4 v 2 shooting corridor

Organisation

The coach marks out a corridor in an arc shape between the penalty spot and the edge of the 'D' (see Figure 11). Four attackers play against two defenders in the corridor. The ball is fed to the strikers by one of two servers positioned outside the shooting corridor. The idea is for the attackers to score as many goals as possible from shots inside the corridor. Players are only allowed out of the corridor to react to rebounds from the goalkeeper. Having made the save the keeper throws the ball to one of the servers.

Key points

- Always expect a shot.
- Adopt a good starting position.
- Cut the diagonal (into line and up the line).
- Steal an extra step forwards as the shooter addresses the ball.
- Be 'set' in the ready position as the ball is struck.
- Use the appropriate saving technique.
- React quickly to make any second saves.

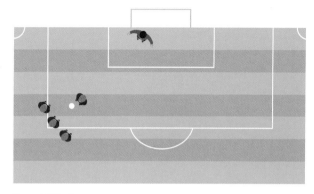

Figure 10 The fan

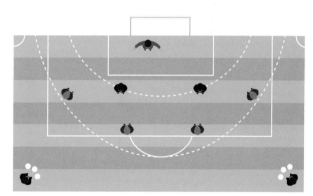

Figure 11 Shooting corridor

SHOT STOPPING
SAVING ON THE MOVE

9

As the game moves so quickly approximately 65 per cent of saves are made while the keeper is on the move

Given that the majority of saves are made while on the move, it is extremely important to recreate situations in training where the keeper is moving forwards, backwards and sideways. If a lack of time prevents the keeper from achieving the set position he should at least be slowing down and try to be balanced as the shot is struck. If his body weight is not evenly distributed it will be impossible for the keeper to change direction. His head, of course, should be still.

(1) Saving in the triangle

Organisation
The keeper stands on one side of a triangle of cones that are 6 yards apart. Two balls are placed 10–12 yards from each side with a server ready to deliver. Having dealt with the first shot, the keeper has to move rapidly to the remaining sides to make saves. He moves twice around the triangle and then rests. While this practice is performed at speed, the server should provide sufficient time for the keeper to execute proper technique. (See photo 41.)

Key points
- Move quickly between goals, trying to keep the feet a shoulder-width apart.
- Lead with the hands as if wearing handcuffs.
- Keep the head steady.
- Use the appropriate saving technique.

Photo 41 Saving in the triangle

(2) Saving on the move – forwards

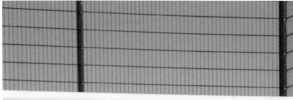

Organisation

There will be occasions during matches when the goalkeeper will not be properly 'set' as the shot is struck. In this exercise the keeper starts in the middle of the goal and moves quickly towards the server who then shoots.

Key points

- Keep the head steady.
- Keep calm and be prepared to improvise a save (the movement will often feel awkward as it is difficult to dive sideways while moving forwards).

(3) Saving on the move – backwards

Organisation

The keeper takes a position 12–18 yards from the goal line. Once the server, who is a further 10–15 yards away, plays the ball out of his feet, the keeper can move backwards into position. The server shoots for goal on his second touch. Progress from central to wide angle positions. (See Figure 12).

Key points

- Take quick, mincing steps backwards.
- Get into line.
- Keep the head steady.
- Keep the body weight forward by ensuring that the line of the shoulders is ahead of the feet.
- Try to be in a 'set' position as the shot is struck.
- Use the appropriate saving technique.

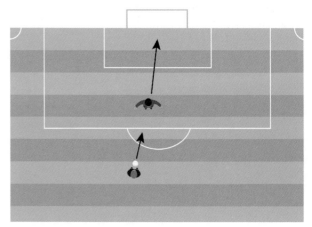

Figure 12 Saving while moving backwards

(4) Changing direction to save

Organisation

The keeper glides to and fro across his goal. As he moves towards one post, the server feeds the ball in the other direction from a distance of 6–10 yards. The goalkeeper has to transfer his body weight to make the save.

Key points

- Do not anticipate the save – glide quickly.
- Glide with the feet a shoulder-width apart.
- When the ball is delivered, dig in and push off from the foot furthest away from the ball.
- Use the appropriate saving technique.

(5) No-hope alley

Organisation

The keeper stands at one post facing out towards the touchline. The server, standing 10–20 yards from the goal line, shouts 'Turn!' Once the keeper has spun round and is starting to cross the goalmouth, the server shoots for the empty corner. Repeat the practice from the other side of the goal. (See Figure 13.) Progress to varying the service so that the shot is not always predictable.

Key points

- Open the body and assess the danger.
- Get into line as quickly as possible.
- If there is time, get up the line.
- If time permits glide with feet a shoulder-width apart, but if necessary run the first few steps.
- Keep the head steady.
- Slow down as the shot is struck.
- Use the appropriate saving method and improvise if necessary.
- React quickly to make any second saves.

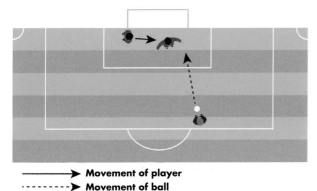

——————▶ **Movement of player**
- - - - - ▶ **Movement of ball**

Figure 13 No-hope alley

(6) Stations

Organisation

Three discs are positioned 8–10 yards from the goal line covering the width of the goal. The keeper is to stand beside one of the discs. As soon as the server, standing 20–22 yards from the goal, plays the ball out of his feet the keeper can move. As the keeper is well out of position and has to recover as quickly as possible he will be forced to save while on the move. (See Figure 14).

Key points

- Move back and into line as quickly as possible.
- If time permits glide with feet a shoulder-width apart, but if necessary run the first few steps.
- Keep the body compact and balanced.
- Keep the head steady.
- Slow down as the shot is struck.
- Use the appropriate saving technique and improvise if necessary.
- React quickly to make any second saves.

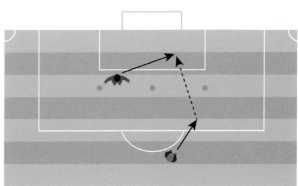

Figure 14 Stations

(7) Even-less-hope alley

Organisation

The goalkeeper takes up a position in the goalmouth as if having made a sprawling save – either lying, sitting or kneeling. As the server, who is positioned just outside the penalty area, plays the ball out of his feet and prepares to shoot, the goalkeeper is allowed to rise to his feet and get into position. The keeper should vary his position each time. (See photos 42a, 42b, 42c and 42d.)

Key points

- Get to the feet as quickly as possible.
- Move into line quickly.
- If time permits glide with feet a shoulder-width apart, but if necessary run the first few steps.
- Keep the head steady.
- Keep the body compact and balanced.
- Slow down as the shot is struck.
- Use the appropriate saving technique and improvise if necessary.
- React quickly to make any second saves.

(8) Gliding across the goal to save

Organisation

The goalkeeper starts from the middle of the goal and glides towards the post. As he does so, the server, standing at the angle of the 6-yard box, shoots for goal. The server should vary the timing and the direction of the shot. An extra player stationed on the middle of the 6-yard line can be used to finish any knock-downs from the keeper (see Figure 15.) The keeper must be aware that if a clean catch is not possible he cannot afford to push the ball weakly into the mid-goal area as it will present any lurking forward with an easy tap-in.

Key points

- Move quickly across the goal.
- Slow down as the striker pulls back the kicking foot.
- If time allows, reduce the striker's shooting angle by getting up the line (i.e. moving towards him).

Photo 42a/b/c/d Even less hope alley

- If possible try to be in the 'set' position as the shot is struck.
- Keep the head steady.
- Be prepared to save with the feet if the ball is delivered low and fast.
- If the shot cannot be gathered cleanly, it should be deflected wide of the far post or parried fiercely away from the goal.

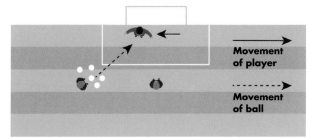

Figure 15 Gliding across the goal to save

SHOT STOPPING
THE IMPERFECT WORLD

10

Always be prepared for the unexpected

The work that a goalkeeper has to cope with is not always straightforward because there is a constantly changing scene in front of him. Teammates as well as opponents make life difficult by blocking his field of vision. There are times when the ball is seen very late; when deflections or cutbacks momentarily catch the keeper out of position; and when opponents use trickery to chip and swerve shots. Often the situation will necessitate some last-minute improvisation on his part. For example, he might use a trailing leg to clear the ball after being wrong-footed by a deflection.

Some people might argue that you cannot coach players to deal with the unexpected because they will act instinctively anyway. However, if in training the coach can recreate these unpredictable situations, the goalkeeper will know how to react when they happen again and, who knows, it might be the save that turns the game.

Dealing effectively with unexpected situations relies on two key ingredients:

1 Attitude. Being determined not to beaten even in seemingly impossible situations.

2 Improvisation. Sometimes the situation simply does not allow for the execution of orthodox technique and the keeper has to be creative.

(1) Forward roll and save

Organisation
The purpose of this practice is to momentarily disorient the goalkeeper and for the shot to be made before he has time to get in the ready position. The goalkeeper stands in the middle of his goal and completes a forward roll. As he is coming out of the roll the server shoots from 10–12 yards. The keeper makes the save. Only perform six repetitions before resting as too many can make the keeper dizzy. Progress to backward rolls.

Key points
- Try to come out of the roll in a compact position ready to change direction at the last moment.
- Keep the head steady.
- Use the appropriate saving technique (but be prepared to improvise using any body part as a barrier).
- React quickly to make any second save.

(2) Saving from a sitting position

Organisation
The keeper sits and on the command 'Up!' gets to his feet. As the keeper rises the server shoots from a distance of 6–10 yards. (See photo 43.)

Photo 43 Saving from a sitting position

75

Key points

- Get up as quickly as possible.
- Keep the head steady.
- Use the appropriate saving technique.
- React quickly to make any second saves.

(3) Saving the chip

Organisation

The goalkeeper sits on his 6-yard line (further out for more experienced players) and the server stands just outside the penalty area. At the first signs of movement from the keeper, the server chips the ball towards the goal. The keeper has to make the save. Sharpen the keeper's competitive edge by recording the score out of ten.

Key points

- Get up quickly.
- Keep the head steady.
- Take rapid, mincing steps backwards before attempting to save.
- Catch or deflect to safety.

(4) The cut back

Organisation

The server starts with the ball on the angle of the penalty area and the keeper reacts to this position. The server moves across the area to a marker, at which he attempts to cut the ball back inside the near post. The practice is repeated from the other side of the area. As the keeper becomes more proficient the server can vary the timing and angle of the shot. (See Figure 16.)

Key points

- Get into line with the ball.
- Glide with the feet a shoulder-width apart and stay balanced.
- Do not be pulled too far across the goal.
- Get up the line if possible.
- Be 'set' in the ready position as the shot is struck.
- Use the appropriate saving method.
- React quickly to make any second saves.

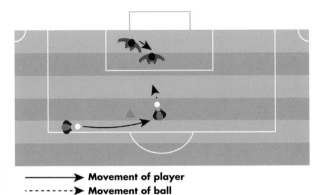

———▶ **Movement of player**
- - - - - ▶ **Movement of ball**

Figure 16 The cut back

(5) Divots (saving deflections off marker discs)

Organisation

This practice is designed to recreate shots that have taken an unexpected bounce off an uneven surface. Ten marker discs are scattered in a central location 4–6 yards from the goal. From a distance of 18–20 yards, the server fires in a ground shot through the discs. On some occasions the ball will hit the disc and change direction and on others the ball will skim through unaffected. The keeper has to deal with either eventuality. (See Figure 17.)

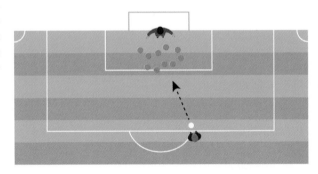

Figure 17 Divots

Key points

- Adopt the ready position.
- Do not get too close to the cones (because it affords less reaction time).
- Keep the head steady.
- Go for the first shot but be prepared to improvise if the ball is deflected.
- Do not panic if the ball is deflected.

(6) Saving deflections off cones

Organisation

In this practice the obstacles placed in front of the goalie present even more of a challenge. Three or four heavy cones are placed 6–8 yards from the goal line. The server shoots from 18–20 yards, aiming to either bend the ball round or deflect it off the cones. The keeper has to save.

Key points

- Adopt the ready position.
- Do not get too close to the cones (because it affords less reaction time).
- Keep the head steady.
- Do not panic if momentarily unsighted or the ball is deflected.
- Go for the first shot but be prepared to improvise if the ball is deflected.

(7) Saving deflections using players

Organisation

This practice is very similar to (6), but this time the cones are replaced by one or two outfield players who can make life difficult by obscuring the keeper's view and deflecting or dummying the ball. These players will capitalise on any loose handling. (See photo 44.)

Photo 44 Saving deflections using players

Key points

- Adopt the ready position.
- Do not be distracted by the player(s) in front.
- Get a view of the ball without compromising the starting position or becoming unbalanced.
- Do not get too close to the player(s) in front.
- Keep the head steady.
- Go for the first shot but be ready to improvise if the ball is deflected.
- React quickly to make any second save.

(8) Saving with the feet

Saving with the feet is recommended when the pace and close proximity of the shot make safe handling impossible. Little back-lift is required because the goalkeeper can easily use the pace on the ball to redirect it to safety.

Organisation

The goalkeeper defends a small goal 1 yard wide. The server shoots low and hard from a distance of 5 yards. The keeper is not allowed to save with the hands and must use the feet or legs. Progress to varying the service and allow the keeper to use the hands when appropriate. (See photo 45.)

Photo 45 Saving with the feet

Key points
- Keep the head steady.
- Keep the legs less than a ball-width apart.
- Turn the feet outwards to present a large barrier.
- Use little back-lift.
- Redirect the ball to safety.

(9) Saving with the feet or hands – barrage

Organisation
The keeper stands on his goal line faced by ten balls placed along the 6-yard box. There is a server at each end. The server at one end fires a shot straight at the keeper. As soon as he has saved, a shot arrives from the second server. The servers should vary the height of the shots. This process continues until all of the balls have been kicked. The service must be rapid but controlled. (See photo 46.)

Photo 46 Saving with the feet or hands – barrage

Key points
- Keep the head steady.
- Adopt the ready position.
- Make the correct decision (to save with the feet or hands).
- Use the correct saving technique.

(10) Blocking without using the hands

Organisation
Occasionally there is no time to save the ball with the hands and the keeper has to use a body part to block the shot or header. This practice recreates this scenario. The keeper kneels on the goal line and on the command of 'Up' the server shoots from 6 yards. The keeper has to use any body part, other than his hands, to block the ball. (See photo 47.)

Photo 47 Blocking without the hands

Key points
- Stay big and keep the head steady.
- Get in line with the ball and present the most appropriate body part as a barrier.
- Quickly make a second save.

(11) Second saves

There will be occasions when shots cannot be dealt with conclusively and the goalkeeper must make a second save. This requires him to rise quickly to provide the best possible chance of dealing with any follow-up shots. Second saves are much easier to perform when the keeper's body weight has been falling forwards in the initial stop.

Organisation
The keeper lies on his front with his head 4 yards from the post.

The server stands 6–8 yards away. On the server's command the keeper rises and the ball is played inside the post. The keeper has to react to prevent the ball from crossing the line. Progress by varying the pace and height of the shot.

Key points
- Rise quickly to provide a platform from which to dive (i.e. wholly or partly on the feet).
- Keep the head steady.
- If necessary, improvise to keep the ball out.
- Do not relax until the ball is safe.

(12) Wrestling to save

Organisation
This practice recreates those situations when the keeper is impeded as he tries to position himself for a shot. The goalkeeper stands in the middle of the goal ready to face a shot from the server standing at the edge of the penalty area. Before the shot is delivered, the keeper is manhandled by another player (preferably of a similar physique) and he has to break free before making the save. The practice is demanding and should be repeated between six to ten times, depending on the level of the performer.

Key points
- Get into position as soon as possible.
- Be prepared to improvise a save if off balance.
- React quickly to make any second save.

(13) Dippers and swervers

Ironically, long shots can present more of a problem than short range ones due to the fact that there is more time for the ball to dip and swerve in flight. The goalkeeper should follow the basic rules of getting in line but must not panic if the ball dips or swerves at the last second. The save might look ungainly but artistic merit is not an objective!

Organisation
The server occupies a position just outside of the penalty area. Using volleys, half-volleys and ground shots, he provides the keeper with a varied bombardment.

Key points
- Get into line and up the line.
- Get 'set' in the ready position as the shot is struck and do not shift the body weight too early.
- Keep the head steady.
- Apply the appropriate saving technique.
- If the ball deviates, stay calm and deflect or parry to safety if a catch is not possible.
- React quickly to make any second save.

(14) Long range shots small-sided game

Organisation
This practice takes place in an area 40 × 40 yards. Each team has three defenders and two attackers. Defenders must remain in their own half and attackers in their opponents' half. The aim is for the defenders to create shooting opportunities for themselves. The attackers try to make it difficult for the opposition by dummying, deflecting and following shots. (See Figure 18.)

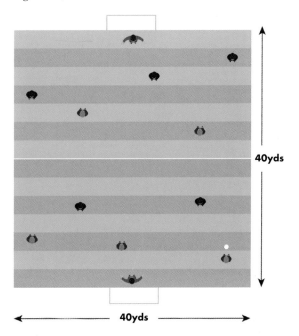

Figure 18 Long range shots small-sided game

Quick reactions are vital to successful goalkeeping

There is a commonly held belief that instinctive elements of skilled performance, such as reaction saves, cannot be coached. This is not entirely true as reaction time can be improved through practice. By rehearsing game-like scenarios in training, the goalkeeper can be more effective in dealing with close range shots and headers. Commentators often mistakenly refer to 'reflex saves' to describe those occasions when the keeper reacts extremely quickly to deal with what appears to be a certain goal. Reaction saves are usually a combination of good technique, agility and improvisation. The technical element will probably involve quick footwork to arrive at the right place at the right time. Agility will be needed to ensure that a body part gets in the way of the ball. An improvised save is likely to be required when there is insufficient time to deal with the shot or header in a more conventional manner.

The most common failing of goalkeepers when faced with a close range shot is the tendency to fall backwards and go to ground. He must stay on his feet to provide the biggest barrier and greatest reach possible. Secondly he must keep his head still with eyes focused on the ball. This is not easy for young goalkeepers to achieve as the natural inclination is to seek evasive action when a player is about to blast the ball goal-wards from short range. By 'staying big' the keeper will be able to fill up the goal and be in a better position to readjust if the initial effort is blocked. Dropping back to the line will increase the reaction time and provide more time to see the ball.

As the speed of the shot or header might not allow the application of conventional saving technique, the keeper must be prepared to improvise and use any body part to keep the ball out of the net. In this case the end justifies the means and the fact that the save may be made with a foot, knee or shoulder is immaterial. As in all cases of course, the keeper should be ready to make a second save if required.

In the split second that the keeper has to react he has to assess whether he is going to block the ball or save it. There is a subtle difference between blocking and saving. Blocking is used when the keeper decides to use his body as a barrier and hopes that the shot hits him and rebounds to safety. Saving involves a deliberate act of using the hands or feet to deal with the shot and is employed when the keeper has more time to see the ball.

(1) Spin and drop

Organisation

The keeper stands with his legs open, facing the server standing 2–3 yards away. The server passes the ball through the keeper's legs and he has to spin and dive to save. The exercise is repeated ten times with the keeper alternating the direction in which he spins.

Key points
- Spin quickly, keeping the head steady.
- Dive with the first hand reaching round the far side of the ball and the second hand on top.
- Pull the ball safely into the body.

(2) Through the legs and drop

Organisation

The keeper stands with his legs open, facing away from the server who stands 2–3 yards away. The server passes the ball through the goalkeeper's legs who dives to save. The exercise is repeated ten times.

Key points
- Dive with the first hand reaching round the far side of the ball and the second hand on top.
- Be prepared to move the feet if the ball is delivered quickly.
- Pull the ball safely into the body.

(3) One touch returns

Organisation
The goalkeeper stands in the goal 6 yards wide with a supply of balls behind him. The keeper rolls the ball out to the server standing 4–6 yards away. The server returns a first time side foot shot at varying heights and angles.

Key points
- React to the shot, do not go to ground too early.
- Keep the head steady.
- Use the appropriate hand shape to gather the ball.
- Be ready to make a second save if required.

(4) Saving from random touches

Organisation
The server stands three yards from the goalkeeper and either bounces the ball off his foot or thigh. This creates an unpredictable rebound for the keeper to save.

Key points
- Stay big to present a large barrier.
- Keep the head steady.
- Do not move too early.
- Improvise the save if necessary.

(5) Through the legs, spin and save

Organisation
The goalkeeper stands in a goal 4 yards wide with his back to the server. He feeds the ball through his legs, spins and prepares to receive a shot from the server standing at varying distances. The keeper alternates the direction in which he spins.

Key points
- Spin quickly with the head steady.
- Stay back to increase reaction time.
- React to the shot, do not go to ground too early.
- Be prepared to improvise if there is insufficient time to gather the ball cleanly.
- Be ready to make a second save if required.

(6) Spin and save

Organisation

The goalkeeper faces the goal. On the command 'Turn!' from the server, who stands at varying distances, he turns to save the shot. The exercise is repeated in sets of ten.

Key points

- Spin quickly with the head steady.
- Get into line and up the line if time allows.
- Be prepared to improvise if there is insufficient time to gather the ball cleanly.
- Be ready to make a second save if required.

(7) The pull back

Organisation

The goalkeeper faces server 1 standing outside the line of the post. He plays a crisp pass to server 2 positioned 6–8 yards from goal. Server 2 moving into the flight of the pass shoots into the near part of the goal. The keeper has to move quickly to face the striker and make the save (see Figure 19). The exercise is repeated in sets of ten.

Key points

- Turn and move across the goal quickly with the head steady.
- Stay back to increase reaction time.
- Choose the appropriate saving technique but be prepared to improvise if necessary.
- Be ready to make a second save if required.

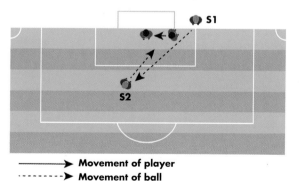

Figure 19 The pull back

(8) Close range volleys

Organisation

The goalkeeper faces server 1 standing outside the line of the post. He feeds by hand to server 2 positioned 4–6 yards from goal. Server 2 side foot volleys the ball towards the near part of the goal.

The keeper has to move quickly to face the striker and make the save (see Figure 20). The exercise is repeated in sets of ten.

Key points

- Turn quickly with the head steady.
- Stay back to increase reaction time.
- Stand up (stay big) to present the body as a barrier.
- Decide whether to block or save.
- Be prepared to improvise if there is insufficient time to gather the ball cleanly.
- Be ready to make a second save if required.

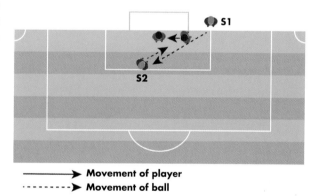

Figure 20 Close range volleys

(9) Close range headers

Organisation

Server 1 stands behind the goalkeeper who faces server 2. Server 1 hand feeds the ball to server 2 who heads for goal from 4–6 yards.

Key points

- Stay back, stay deep.
- Be prepared to improvise a block if there is insufficient time to gather the ball cleanly.
- Be ready to make a second save if required.

(10) Reaction saves through the legs of defenders

Organisation

With the goalkeeper on his goal line, one or two players stand on the 6-yard line with their legs open. From a distance of 10 yards the server shoots for goal aiming through the legs of the two players. (See photo 48.)

Key points

- Stay back, stay big.
- Stay balanced with the head steady.
- Improvise if necessary.
- Be ready to make a second save if required.

Photo 48 Reactions through the legs

(11) Reaction saves past the bodies of defenders

Organisation

With the goalkeeper on his goal line, a player stands on the 6-yard line obscuring the view of the keeper. From a distance of 10 yards the server volleys past the defender's head and upper body.

Key points

As in (9) above.

(12) The heading game

Organisation

The practice takes place with two small (4 × 2 yard) goals 6 yards apart. With a goalkeeper in each goal the server feeds the ball so that one keeper has to execute a diving header for goal. The other goalkeeper has to make a reaction save and then it is his turn for a header. This game is immense fun and has enormous benefit for the goalkeeper's competiveness, reaction saves and agility.

Key points

- Stay back, stay big.
- Improvise if necessary.
- Be ready to make a second save if required.

(13) Reaction saves small-sided game

Organisation

The game takes place on a pitch 18 × 18 yards with a goal at each end. Each team has a goalkeeper, two players and feeders positioned either side of the opponent's goal. To achieve a strike or header, the ball has to be passed to the feeder who plays the ball first time for a shot or throws it in for a header. After three minutes, rotate the players and feeders. (See Figure 21.)

Key points

- Adjust the position in relation to the ball.
- Stay back, stay big.
- Stay balanced with the head steady.
- Decide whether to save or block.
- Be ready to make a second save if required.

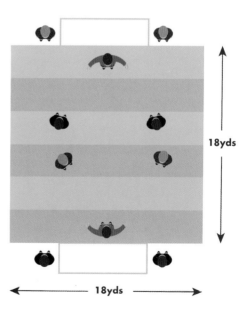

18yds

18yds

Figure 21 Reaction saves small-sided game

With the exception of saving a penalty, the closest a goalkeeper can get to scoring a goal is to save in a 1 v 1 situation

By preventing the player from scoring a certain goal, the keeper can lift his teammates and demoralise the opposition. Saving in 1 v 1 situations more often than not requires good judgement combined with raw courage and a disregard for personal safety. However, if the technique is executed properly and with conviction, injury to the goalkeeper seldom results. Everyone expects a goal to be scored when a player is clear of the defence – that is, everyone except the keeper! It is essential that he is mentally aggressive and is determined not to be beaten. If a goal is going to be conceded, he must make the opponent earn his reward.

When the ball is played in behind the defence or when the attacker breaks through, the goalkeeper must resist the temptation to react instinctively and instead, rapidly weigh up the situation. He has three choices – to win, block or save the ball. His judgement will be based on playing the percentages and making life as difficult as possible for the ball carrier.

In all 1 v 1 situations the goalkeeper must take great care not to foul the opponent because the double punishment of a penalty kick conceded and dismissal from the field usually follows. For this reason, the keeper's reading of the situation, his decision and his saving technique must be perfect.

If the opponent has good control of the ball, it is not advisable for the keeper to rush him. By committing himself when there is little chance of winning possession or blocking the shot, the keeper will only succeed in making life easier for the ball carrier. Once the keeper goes to ground he is momentarily out of the game so he should stay on his feet unless he is sure of winning or blocking the ball.

As the ball carrier approaches he is under pressure because a goal is expected, and he is further stressed by the numerous alternatives open to him. Does he take the ball round the keeper? Attempt a chip, a side-foot shot or a blast? The keeper who rushes impetuously in this situation makes up the mind of the opponent, who will neatly side-step the rash lunge and put the ball into the net.

If the player has close control of the ball, the keeper must stay on his feet in an attempt to 'buy' himself time and, better still, force his opponent wide so that the shooting angle is reduced. In these situations the keeper should be wary of a low shot past his feet and should therefore bend the knees and keep the hands held low in the 'gate' position (see photo 49). A very high percentage of goals conceded in 1 v 1 situations result from shots going through the keeper's legs and the 'gate' position helps to counteract this. At the same time recovering defenders should be encouraged to get across the path of the ball carrier in order to reduce his options.

Photo 49 The gate position

The following scenarios may help to clarify the most appropriate course of action:

Scenario 1: the ball is played into space behind the defence

ASSESSMENT
The keeper assesses the relative distances that he and the nearest opponent are to the ball.

DECISION
Based on the assessment that at best he is going to get to the ball first or at worst at approximately the same time as the opponent, the keeper decides to attack and moves quickly without hesitation. In the last few paces he chooses to either win or block the ball.

TECHNIQUE
To win possession the goalkeeper dives into the path of the ball and, with one hand behind and the other on top, traps it. As the ball is collected it is quickly brought into the chest. He provides further protection by tucking in the head and legs. To block the ball the keeper can use one of two techniques. The spreading block, which is used when the keeper and opponent arrive at the same time, entails leading with the hands and spreading his body to present the widest barrier possible (see photo 54 on page 91). To counteract skilful opponents who will try to lift the ball over the diving body, the keeper can raise the top arm. To execute the upright block, which is used when the opponent is clearly going to get to the ball first, the keeper drops one knee with the leg turned sideways and extends his hands either side of the body. This provides a barrier that is tall and also wide at the base (see photo 50).

Photo 50 The upright block

Scenario 2: the opponent dribbles through the defence

ASSESSMENT
The keeper assesses the ball carrier's control.

DECISION (A)
The keeper recognises that the opponent's last touch is heavy and he has momentarily lost control. The keeper decides to advance quickly to either win the ball outright or to execute a block.

TECHNIQUE (A)
The keeper responds as in scenario 1.

DECISION (B)
The keeper realises that the ball carrier has good control and decides to buy time for fellow defenders to recover and to put pressure on the opponent.

TECHNIQUE (B)
The keeper advances cautiously and narrows the angle trying to force the opponent wide. He stays on his feet and prepares to save the shot. The opponent is likely to shoot hard and low close to the keeper, so it is recommended that he keeps a low ready position and is prepared to save with the feet.

Scenario 3: the ball breaks to an unmarked opponent very close to the goal

ASSESSMENT
The keeper judges the degree of immediate danger.

DECISION
As there is very little time, the keeper decides to rush the opponent in order to block the shot.

TECHNIQUE
The keeper advances rapidly and executes an upright blocking technique to present the largest possible barrier. The ploy is to induce panic in the opponent and make him rush his shot.

(1) Diving at feet from a kneeling, crouching and standing position

Organisation
These progressive practices are designed to introduce young players to diving at an opponent's feet in a way that induces confidence. As the keeper kneels, the server walks past on the right and left sides with the ball at his feet. Progress to the keeper crouching and then standing with the server running with the ball. (See photo 51.)

Photo 51 Diving at feet, side-on

Key points
- Time the dive correctly – take the ball, not the player.
- Lead with the hands.
- Keep the head steady and the eyes open.
- Claim the ball with one hand behind and one on top.
- Pull the ball into the chest.
- Tuck in the head and legs for additional protection.

(2) Head first diving at feet

Organisation
As in practice (1) but this time the server approaches the goalkeeper head-on. (See photo 52.)

Photo 52 Diving at feet, head-on

Key points
- Time the dive correctly – take the ball, not the player.
- Lead with the hands.
- Keep the head steady and the eyes open.
- First hand reaches round the front of the ball, second hand on top of the ball.
- Pull the ball into the chest.
- Tuck in the head and legs for additional protection.

(3) 2 v 1 saving at feet

Organisation

This practice combines decision making with the appropriate technique. Two players and one goalkeeper play in a grid measuring 10 × 10 yards. The players attempt to keep possession while the keeper aims either to claim the ball, or to divert it, out of the grid. The keeper is allowed to attack the ball after the first pass. After gaining five successes the goalkeeper rests. (See Figure 22.)

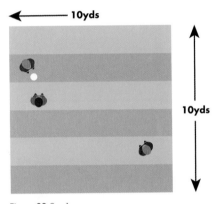

Figure 22 2 v 1

Key points

- Advance to narrow the angle and put the player under pressure.
- Adopt a low ready position (the gate) with the hands by the side of the feet.
- Assess the situation, looking for any errors in control.
- Stay on the feet unless sure of winning the ball.
- Threaten the ball carrier by feinting to dive.
- Try to manoeuvre the ball carrier into a tight space (for example, a corner or a line).
- When winning the ball, lead with the hands.
- When blocking use either the spreading or upright technique.
- Be committed with the head steady and the eyes open.
- Do not foul.

(4) 1 v 1 winning the ball

Organisation

In a grid measuring 10 × 10 yards the server has to round the keeper to score into a goal 3 yards wide. (See photo 53.)

Photo 53 winning the ball

Key points

- Advance to narrow the angle and put the player under pressure.
- Adopt a low ready position with the hands by the sides of the feet.
- Stay on the feet until sure of winning the ball.
- Try to force the ball carrier away from the goal.
- Look to attack if the player miscontrols the ball.
- When diving, lead with the hands.
- Be committed with the head steady and the eyes open.
- Do not foul.

(5) The upright block

Organisation

Six balls are placed in an arc 2 yards from the goal. As the server moves towards the ball, the keeper has to advance to block the shot. The goalkeeper then returns to his starting position and the exercise is repeated.

Key points

- Cover the ground quickly.
- Drop one knee with the leg turned sideways.
- Extend the hands on either side of the body.
- Stay big and use the body as a barrier.
- Keep the head steady with eyes focused on the ball.

(6) The spreading block

Organisation

Server 1 is positioned 3 yards wide of the 6-yard line while server 2 stands between 6–8 yards from the goal line. Server 1 plays to Server 2 who is conditioned to shoot on his second touch. Server 2 has a heavy first touch so that the goalkeeper is able to attack the ball leading with his hands.

Key points

- Close down the shooter quickly as the ball is travelling and assess whether to win the ball outright or block it.
- If winning the ball lead with both hands.
- If the shooter gets to the ball first, spread the hands to provide the biggest possible barrier (see photo 54).
- Be committed and keep the eyes open.
- Get up quickly to make a second save if required.

Photo 54 The spreading block

(7) 1 v 1 winning or blocking the ball

Organisation

The purpose of this practice is to help the keeper to make the appropriate decision on whether to win or block the ball. In a grid measuring 10 × 10 yards the keeper throws a fast ball to the server who controls it to score into a goal 3 yards wide. The server can score with a side foot shot or by dribbling around the keeper. If the server's first touch is poor, the keeper will have the opportunity to attack the ball. On the other hand, if his control is good, then staying on the feet is recommended. The server should vary his starting position to test the goalkeeper's understanding of how to force the ball carrier wide.

Key points

- Advance to put the opponent under pressure.
- Assess the opponent's first touch.
- If winning the ball, lead with the hands.
- If blocking, choose the appropriate technique.
- If unsure of winning the ball, stay on the feet.
- Put pressure on the opponent.
- Try to force the opponent wide.
- Be prepared to save with the feet if necessary.

(8) Plunging

Organisation

This practice is useful in building up a young goalkeeper's confidence and competence in 'going in where it hurts'. The server stands 6 yards from the goal line with a player on either side. The goalkeeper stands on the line facing the server who feeds the ball between the keeper and one of the players (see Figure 23). The service should be rolled or bounced so that the keeper has to deal with balls at varying heights. Depending on his proximity to the ball, the keeper has to decide to claim it outright or to execute a block.

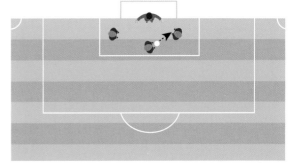

Figure 23 Plunging

Key points

- Decide whether to win the ball or block.
- Be committed and keep the eyes open whatever the course of action.
- If attempting to win the ball, lead with the hands.
- If blocking, use the spreading block technique.
- Be prepared to make a second save if necessary.

(9) The through ball

Organisation

From a distance of 35 yards from goal, the coach plays the ball in front of an attacking player (standing 25–30 yards from goal) who has to score. The coach can vary the pace, length and angle of the pass to test the keeper's judgement of when to attack the ball and when to hold his ground. (See Figure 24.)

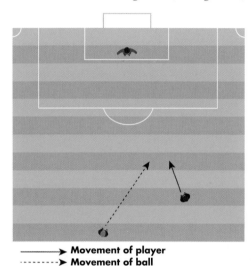

──────► **Movement of player**
------► **Movement of ball**

Figure 24 The through ball

Key points

• Adopt a good starting position (advanced enough to intercept an overhit ball, but not so far as to be vulnerable to the chip).
• Assess the situation.
• Make the correct decision to win, block or save.
• Employ the appropriate technique.

(10) The shoot-out

Organisation

The ball carrier sets off from a predetermined point (either centrally or at an angle) 35 yards from goal with a defender in pursuit starting 5 yards behind him. The goalkeeper and defender have to deal with the situation. The coach can vary the starting position of the attackers and defenders to recreate game situations. (See Figure 25.)

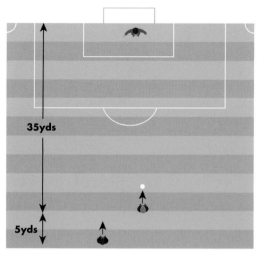

35yds

5yds

Figure 25 The shoot-out

Key points

• Adopt a good starting position (advanced enough to intercept an overhit ball, but not too far off the line to be vulnerable to the chip).
• Assess the ball carrier's control and the position of the defender.
• If the ball carrier has good ball control come down the line cautiously to narrow the angle and put the player under pressure.
• Put the player off by feinting to threaten the ball.
• Try to force the opponent wide.
• If attempting to win the ball, lead with the hands.
• If blocking, use the spreading or upright blocking technique.
• Be prepared to save with the feet if necessary.
• Maintain good communication with the recovering defender.

(11) Breaking into the penalty area

Organisation

A 15 × 10 yard rectangle is marked out just outside on the penalty area. Three attackers and one defender are positioned in the rectangle, and once the server has played the ball in, the attackers have to either use some combination play or an individual dribble to break into the penalty area to finish. Only one attacking player is allowed into the area at which point the defender is permitted to follow and challenge him. (See Figure 26.)

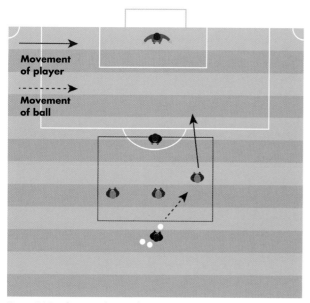

Figure 26 Breaking into the penalty area

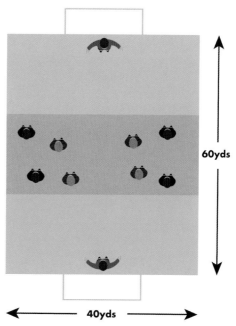

Figure 27 Breakout SSG

Key points

- Adopt a good starting position and always expect a shot.
- Assess the intention of the attackers.
- Make the correct decision to win, block or save. If the ball carrier has control, 'buy' time and force him wide.
- When winning the ball, lead with the hands and be committed.
- When blocking, stay big and use the body as a barrier.
- Do not foul.

(12) Small-sided game – breakout

Organisation

The practice takes the form of a small-sided game (four against four including two goalkeepers) in an area measuring 60 × 40 yards. For the purpose of the practice, the pitch is divided into three equal sections and outfield players are restricted to the middle third of the pitch unless the ball is either played into one of the end zones or a player dribbles through into one of the end zones. Only one player from each team is allowed to enter the end zone. The aim of the practice is to give the keeper experience of realistic 1 v 1 situations. (See Figure 27.)

Key points

- Adopt a good starting position and always expect a shot.
- Be ready to intercept through-balls.
- Assess the situation.
- Make the correct decision.
- If the ball carrier has good control, 'buy' time and force him wide.
- When diving at feet, lead with the hands and be committed.
- When blocking, stay big and use the body as a barrier.
- Do not foul.
- Be prepared to save close shots with the feet.
- Maintain good communication with the recovering defender.

SHOT STOPPING
SAVING PENALTIES

13

With the results of so many matches, even World Cup Finals, being decided on penalties, the technique of saving them has assumed greater significance in the modern game

As in 1 v 1 situations, the pressure during penalty kicks is on the player and not the goalkeeper since, once the ball is placed on the spot, a goal is the expected outcome. Furthermore, during penalty shoot-outs the stress on the penalty taker is even greater, especially when the scores are close. This is particularly true for those players who are not the regular penalty taker. For this reason, the keeper might wish to adopt different strategies to suit the situation. There are two basic techniques: gambling by moving early, or standing up to react to the shot.

MOVING EARLY

The reason why the goalkeeper moves early is because a shot aimed into the corner with pace will otherwise be impossible to save. There are a number of ploys that the keeper can use to assist this guesswork.

Assessing the type of player taking the kick

Generally speaking, defenders take fewer risks than midfield or forward players and tend to play safe by pushing the ball to the same side as the kicking foot. Tricky, skilful players may try to fool the goalkeeper by clipping the ball to the opposite side of the kicking foot.

Trying to 'dummy' the kicker

As the player runs up to take the kick, the keeper feints to move in one direction. The object is to make the kicker think that the keeper is going to dive that way. As a result he places the ball on the other side – right into the arms of the keeper.

Moving backwards and forwards along the goal line

By moving to and fro along the goal line the keeper may put the player off and cause him to misdirect the shot. However, it must be remembered that it is very difficult to dive in one direction while moving in the other!

Standing on one side of the goal

Standing slightly to one side of the centre of the goal may also disrupt the concentration of the kicker who may be forced to change his original intention. It is a brave player who will elect to direct the shot towards the smaller part of the goal. So the goalkeeper should gamble and move to cover the bigger gap.

Observing the approach of the kicker

The run-up of the kicker can give some idea of his body position as he strikes the ball and, therefore, an indication of its intended destination. (See Figure 28.) If the player addresses the ball from head-on and a very straight approach (A), then it is highly unlikely that he will be able to play the ball to the same side as the kicking foot. The shot will either be delivered straight or swung across the body into the opposite corner. If the approach is curved (B), the kicker is likely to shoot to the same side as the kicking foot. From an angled but fairly straight run-up (C), the shot is likely to be placed back across the keeper.

REACTING TO THE SHOT

During normal play it is likely that the keeper will face the regular penalty taker who will probably have a tried-and-tested approach and sufficient composure to execute an accurate shot. However, in the shoot-out as the pressure mounts, the taker may lose his nerve and his aim. Indeed, personal research of many penalty shoot-out situations has indicated that the majority of shots are played towards the centre of the goal. The keeper should play the percentages and concentrate on defending the middle 6 yards of the goal; the temptation to dive early should be resisted in favour of reacting to the shot. (See Figure 29.)

Whatever saving method is used, it would be unrealistic to expect success every time. Experience will indicate which is the most effective strategy and the keeper should persevere with it. The goalkeeper should, of course, practise the various saving methods, but it is difficult to recreate the tension of real match situations during training sessions since the penalty takers will be fairly relaxed in their approach and be therefore more prepared to take risks.

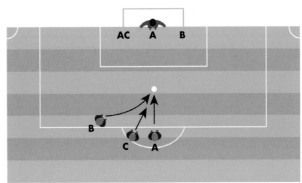

Figure 28 Observing the approach of a right-footed kicker

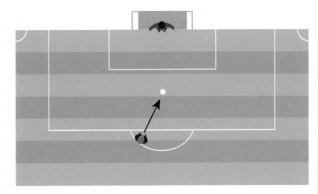

Figure 29 Reading the shot, defending the middle 6 yards

Dealing with the high cross is the yardstick by which top goalkeepers are measured

This is without doubt the most difficult aspect of goalkeeping, since it requires crucial decision-making combined with the application of good technique under physical and mental pressure. As a large percentage of goals result from high balls played into the penalty area, a keeper's worth is often measured in terms of his ability to deal effectively with crosses.

Goalkeepers who consistently come to gather crosses are always very popular with their teammates because it makes their job much easier. However, while no one would appreciate a keeper who never leaves his line, the keeper who has a cavalier approach and goes for every cross can also become a liability.

The goalkeeper must work with his fellow defenders to deal effectively with the ball played into the box. Myths such as 'Every cross into the 6-yard box must be the goalkeeper's' raise unrealistic expectations. Sometimes defenders may be better placed to deal with the problem, such as on near post corners or low-driven crosses.

Nevertheless, the keeper must realise that he has a responsibility to use the advantage that the laws of the game allow him in order to claim those crosses within his range. Of course there will be the odd error of judgement, or days when conditions are not conducive to good handling. However, he must be mentally tough and demonstrate complete faith in his ability to deal effectively with the situation.

On those occasions when confidence is low, he must convince himself that as he has taken hundreds of crosses in the past he can do it again. Furthermore, a shaky, hesitant goalkeeper who does not accept his responsibilities will unsettle defenders and inspire opponents. The coach plays a crucial role in this regard by recreating in training the types of crosses that his goalkeeper is likely to face in matches. This will entail dealing with balls played in from a variety of angles and distances, with varying pace and degree of difficulty.

The high cross can be delivered in three basic ways:

1 In-swinging/out-swinging

2 Floated

3 Driven

Practices should be unopposed until the keeper has mastered the following stages:

- Starting position.
- Working with and organising his defence.
- Assessing the flight and pace of the ball.
- Decision making – to come or stay.
- Communicating the decision.
- The technique of dealing with the cross – catch, punch or deflect.

STARTING POSITION

Adopting the correct starting position is crucial to making good decisions on whether to come for the ball or stay back. When the ball is wide and about to be crossed, the goalkeeper's starting position is critical, since a yard either way can mean the difference between being close enough to attack the ball or being out of range. If the ball is wide, the keeper should start from a position slightly behind the centre of the goal. The reason for this is that it is easier to take the ball moving forwards than backwards. A keeper starting too close to the near post will be struggling to deal with a deep cross. As the ball carrier nears the goal, the keeper should move towards his near post to cover a possible shot. (See Figures 30 and 31.)

Photo 55 Starting position

For those high balls delivered from central positions, typically when the opposition is chasing the game towards the end of the match, the keeper's starting position is just as crucial. In this instance his position will be more central, with the distance from the goal line being proportionate to the distance the ball is from the goal.

Where possible the keeper should also adopt an open stance.

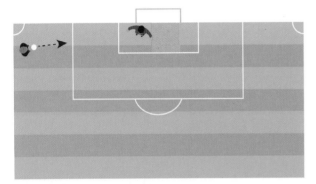

Figures 30 Incorrect starting position

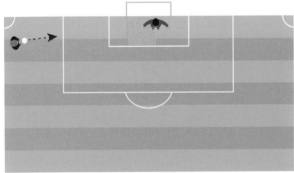

Figures 31 Correct starting position

The keeper's starting position is also related to the proximity of the crosser. The further the crosser is from the goal area, the greater the distance the keeper should be from his goal line. This advanced starting position will extend his range and thereby increase his effectiveness. (See photo 55.)

The open stance serves three purposes:

1 The keeper is in a good position to move rapidly forwards if the situation demands.

2 He is facing play if a cross is whipped in and he has to make a reaction save.

3 It allows him to be aware of the movement of opponents behind him. A closed body position denies him this fuller field of vision.

Working with and organising the defence

The goalkeeper can make the job of dealing with crosses easier by creating space for himself. By discouraging his fellow defenders from dropping too deep around him, he will force opponents to take up positions away from the goal. In other words, if he instructs his teammates to hold their line at the edge of the penalty area, the opposition will not be able to make early runs into the danger area for fear of being offside.

The point at which the defence holds its line will depend on the position of the ball. Generally, the further the ball is from the goal, the higher the line. If executed effectively, the keeper will create space for himself in which he can attack the ball under minimal pressure (see the shaded area in Figure 32). Furthermore, if the opponent does connect with the cross, the header or shot is delivered from a safer distance.

The goalkeeper is in the best position to make the decision of where to hold the line. Teams should practise defending the penalty area in training and agree upon certain responses to a range of given situations. The goalkeeper, through a loud call, should communicate the response. This should be brief (such as 'Up to the spot' or 'Hold the edge') and clearly understood by his colleagues.

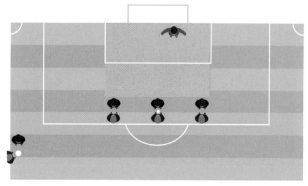

Figure 32 Holding lines

There are four prerequisites for effectively holding the line:

1 The crosser must always be put under pressure to reduce the quality of the cross.

2 The line should not leave too much space for the keeper to deal with.

3 All defending players must move as one to form a uniform line.

4 The keeper should take up an advanced position ready to attack the ball when it is delivered in behind the defence.

It is recommended that the goalkeeper understands where to hold the line. There are five easy points of reference:

1 The 'D'.

2 The edge of the penalty area.

3 The penalty spot.

4 The 6-yard line.

5 Level with the ball.

Generally speaking, if the ball is cleared or passed towards the opponents' goal, the defence should look to move out to compress play. The extent of this movement will depend on the length of the clearance or pass. If the clearance falls to a teammate or forces the opposition to turn and chase the ball, the defence can push up quickly to condense play. However, if the clearance drops to an opponent and there is a danger of the ball being rebounded behind the defence, the defenders should only move out gradually with pressure being applied to the ball carrier.

Assessing the flight and pace of the ball

Although it sounds obvious, the goalkeeper must assess the ball's flight and pace before moving. The many distractions around him, such as his defenders, opponents and his own expectations of where he thinks the ball will be played, will tempt him to anticipate the cross. This type of gambling can prove disastrous. Indeed, the most common cause of a keeper missing a cross is that he moves his feet before reading the ball's flight and pace. He must treat every cross on its own merit and not commit himself before the ball is kicked.

Generally, for crosses that are driven in, the keeper must move fast and win the race to the ball. For crosses floated in, he must arrive late so that he is not caught underneath the ball. By making his attack at the last possible moment, he will be able to use a running jump and, as he will be aware of the players challenging him, his decision to catch or punch will be more reliable. Getting caught underneath the ball can create a problem as it will force the keeper to use a standing jump which does not achieve the same elevation as a one-foot take-off.

Decision making

Having assessed the flight of the ball, the keeper must elect to either stay on his line or to attack the ball. This decision is based on the ball's trajectory, pace and distance from the goal line, as well as the proximity of other players. If, in the keeper's judgement, he has sufficient time to deal safely with the situation, then he should come for the cross. If he has decided not to go for the cross, the keeper should remain on his line and not be drawn to the ball. By stepping back to the line, the keeper might 'buy' himself that extra split-second in which to make a reaction save. In following the ball, the keeper can be caught in 'no man's land' and be vulnerable to the looping header beyond him. For crosses driven or swung into the near-post area, the goalkeeper should move quickly to cover the front half of the goal as this is the likely destination of a quick snap shot or header.

After electing to come for the cross, it is essential that the keeper makes contact with the ball. From the time he decides to go for the cross, his intention must be to catch the ball because that will effectively end the attack. However, at the last moment he must reappraise the situation and decide whether to catch, punch or deflect the ball. This decision is based on how confident the keeper is of making a safe catch.

If the pressure from opponents between the keeper and the ball makes safe handling unlikely, then the keeper should attempt to punch the ball. When the ball is swinging in towards the crossbar, making catching difficult, the keeper should deflect it over the bar for a corner. Similarly, if the goalkeeper is back-pedalling beyond the back post and cannot reach the ball with two hands, he should deflect the ball to safety.

Communicating the decision

The keeper should communicate with his defenders every time the ball is played into the penalty area. As far as crosses are concerned, if the keeper decides to come he should call 'Keeper's!' and if he elects to stay he should call 'Away!' The keeper should call early so that his teammates have time to react. A late call can confuse players who are already committed to a course of action.

In addition, the way in which the keeper communicates is important. His calls must be loud, clear and positive. Defenders will be unsettled by hesitant or panic-stricken instructions. The keeper must give the impression that he is calm and in control of the situation. A good confident call is often the prelude to a good confident catch. A keeper who exudes confidence will inspire and set the tone for the rest of the defence.

THE TECHNIQUE OF DEALING WITH THE CROSS

Having assessed the flight, decided to come for the cross and then communicated his intention to teammates, the keeper must look to gather the ball at the highest safest point. By not attacking the ball there is a danger of opponents getting to it first. Some goalkeepers make the mistake of moving perpendicularly from the line to the cross instead of moving diagonally into the flight of the ball to take it earlier and at the highest safest point. (See Figure 33.) With the benefit of a good starting position, more often than not, the keeper will take the cross moving forwards. He should take off from one foot, bringing up the other leg to give extra lift and some protection against opponents' challenges. If a cross is a deep one, the keeper should move backwards quickly using little mincing steps before taking off from one foot.

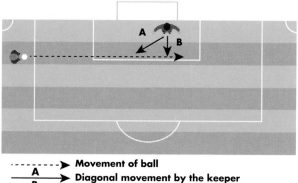

┄┄┄┄► **Movement of ball**
─── **A** ───► **Diagonal movement by the keeper**
─── **B** ───► **Perpendicular movement by the keeper**

Figure 33 *Moving into flight of the ball to catch*

Catching

The goalkeeper must always expect to be challenged when moving out to collect a cross. In this way he will brace his body for physical contact and not be taken by surprise when it occurs. He should avoid locking out the arms directly above the head when catching as he will not be able to see the ball into the hands and it can be easily dislodged under an aggressive challenge. Catching the ball using the W hand shape with arms slightly bent affords a much stronger grip. Extra soft hands are required for those crosses that suddenly drop short at the last moment.

Having made a successful catch, it may not be necessary to bring the ball into the chest because during a match this might be an opportune moment to launch a counter-attack with a fast throw. On the other hand if the keeper's team needs a respite he should bring the ball into the chest and take his time.

It goes without saying that a catch is preferable to a punch, but the keeper must weigh up the risk factors and choose the safer option.

It is recommended that the goalkeeper makes his catch in front of the body and above the head.

Catching in front of the body and above the head serves three purposes:

1. It allows the keeper to see the ball into his hands.

2. By using his arms as shock absorbers, it provides some margin for error if any mishandling occurs.

3. It offers greater leverage if at the last moment he decides to punch. (See photo 56.)

Photo 56 Catching a high cross

Punching

While catching the ball is always the best outcome, it is essential that the goalkeeper understands when and where it is safe to do so. When a safe catch is not possible the keeper should be able to control (by either punching or deflecting) where the ball goes. If the decision is to punch, then the keeper must aim for height, distance and width. When combined, these factors give defenders time to deal with the next wave of attack. Ideally, the keeper should look to punch the ball out of the danger area. For balls swinging in towards the keeper, a punch should be made with two hands because the wider surface area provides a more reliable contact. (See photo 57.) Although using one fist will provide greater reach and may be necessary in emergencies, it can result in a poor connection because the striking surface is narrow and often the keeper is hitting across the body. One-handed punches are more appropriate than the double-fisted clearance when the ball is moving away from the keeper. (See photo 58.)

Effective punching is all about timing and correct hand and ball contact. In order to achieve maximum height and distance in his punch, the keeper should use the flat part of the fist and strike through the bottom half of the ball. The movement should be more of a jab than a swing. He should avoid clenching the fist too tightly as this makes the striking surface uneven and it will result in a mistimed punch. By keeping the wrists rigid it will be possible to transfer maximum power from the forearms into the punch. It is of course essential that the keeper can punch equally well with both fists.

Deflecting

If the ball is swinging in dangerously close to the crossbar and a safe catch is unlikely, the keeper should attempt to turn the ball over the bar using the fingers as they provide greater reach and more sensitivity than the fist. He can employ one of two techniques depending on which one is more comfortable in the circumstances. He can either use the closed technique using the hand furthest from the goal line with the wrist rotating forwards or the open technique using the nearest hand with a backward movement. Care should be taken in ensuring that the touch achieves elevation in order to get the ball over the crossbar (see photo 59a and 59b).

The same open or close-hand techniques are recommended when the keeper is back-pedalling beyond the back post and is unable to catch the ball. The ball should be deflected over the line for a corner. Once committed to the cross it is absolutely imperative that the keeper makes contact with the ball. At best, the goalkeeper should catch and, at worst, he should try to alter the flight path of the ball. Opponents coming in behind the keeper will be following the path of the ball and a deflection might distract them and prevent a clean header.

Since collecting a high cross is an advanced skill, coaches should not expect perfect catches from young boys and girls. Most children below the age of 12 do not possess the hand size or strength to consistently catch a high ball. Therefore, it is quite acceptable for goalkeepers of that age to soft parry the ball first

Photo 57 Two-fisted punching technique

Photo 58 One-handed punching technique

Photos 59a and 59b Helping the ball over the bar, open and closed-hand technique

and to follow up quickly with a second save. When introducing the high cross it is recommended that the service is thrown rather than kicked.

(1) Catching a high ball moving forwards

Organisation
From a distance of 10 yards the server throws the ball high into the air so that the keeper moves forwards to catch it.

Key points
• Assess the flight and pace of the ball.
• Take off on one foot.
• Catch the ball on the way up.
• Take the ball at the highest safest point so that it is in front of the eye-line (using the 'W' hand shape and the forearms as shock absorbers).
• Counter-attack by throwing the ball back quickly to the server.

(2) Catching a high ball moving backwards

Organisation
From a distance of 6 yards the server feeds the ball over the keeper's head so that he has to move quickly backwards to make the catch. The keeper should practise moving backwards using a sideways glide as well as square-on.

Key points
• Assess the flight and pace of the ball.
• Take quick, mincing steps backwards.
• Take off from one foot.
• Catch the ball at the highest safest point so that it is in front of the eye-line (using the 'W' hand shape and the forearms as shock absorbers).
• Counter-attack by throwing the ball quickly to the server.
• If off-balance while moving backwards, go to ground.

(3) Catching from varied service

Organisation
From a distance of 10 yards and a variety of angles the server throws the ball across the face of the goal. The service is varied so that the keeper takes some balls going forwards and others going backwards.

Key points
• Adopt a good starting position (backwards from centre).
• Take up a sideways stance.
• Assess the flight and pace of the ball.
• Take off on one foot.
• Catch the ball on the way up.
• Take the ball at the highest safest point (using the 'W' hand shape and forearms as shock absorbers).
• Counter-attack by throwing the ball quickly to the server.

(4) Catching the ball from a standing jump

Organisation
This practice attempts to recreate the situation when the keeper is caught underneath the ball and is forced into a two-footed take-off. The server stands by the side of the goalkeeper and throws the ball directly up into the air. The keeper has to take off from where he stands to catch the ball. Progress to the server challenging the keeper as he goes to catch.

Key points
• Assess the flight of the ball.
• Take off from two feet.
• Catch the ball on the way up.
• Catch the ball at the highest safest point (using the 'W' hand shape and forearms as shock absorbers).
• Brace the body for a challenge.
• Go to ground if off-balance.

(5) Basketball

Organisation

This practice is designed to prepare the keeper for the physical challenges he can expect in a game situation. The practice can take the form of a 3 v 3 or 4 v 4 in a grid measuring 15 × 15 yards. Each team must keep possession via throws passed above head height. Five consecutive passes caught above head height constitute a goal. The participants are not allowed to run with the ball or prevent an opponent from passing. Possession may only be gained via an interception.

Key points

- Assess the flight and pace of the ball.
- Catch the ball at the highest safest point (using the 'W' hand shape and forearms as shock absorbers).
- Brace the body for a challenge.

(6) Catch or punch

Having mastered a range of punching techniques via practices (14) to (17) (see page 110–111), the keeper should practice when and where to use them.

Organisation

As in (3) but an opponent stands in front of the goalkeeper and challenges for the ball. The server varies the trajectory and pace of the ball so that the keeper has to decide whether to catch or punch. Progress to head-on service. (See photos 60a and 60b.)

Photo 60a and 60b Catch or punch

Key points

- Adopt a good starting position (backwards from centre).
- Take up a sideways stance.
- Assess the flight (react to the ball, not to the movement of the opponent).
- Take off from one foot to take the ball at the highest point.
- If the trajectory is low, win the race to the ball. If the ball is hung up, go late.
- Brace the body for a challenge.
- Decide whether to catch or punch at the last moment.
- Use the 'W' hand shape and forearms as shock absorbers if looking to catch.
- If punching, aim for height, distance and width. Use two hands for the in-swinging ball and one hand for the ball across the body.

(7) Dealing with kicked service (without opposition)

Organisation

Having dealt effectively with hand service, it is now appropriate to move to a more realistic practice where crosses are kicked in. The novice keeper will initially experience problems because catching properly delivered crosses is much more difficult than dealing with thrown balls. Once the keeper is comfortable dealing with kicked crosses, the server can vary the service. This includes:

- Three different angles – one close to the goal line, another 10 yards from the goal line and the third level with the edge of the penalty area. (See Figure 34.)
- In-swinging and out-swinging crosses.
- Driven and floated deliveries

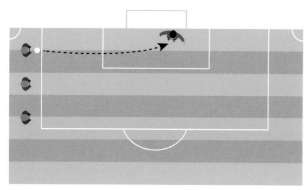

Figure 34 Kicked service from various angles

Key points

- Adopt a good starting position in relation to the near post and the goal line (depending on the position of the ball.)
- Take up a sideways stance.
- Assess the flight and pace of the ball.
- Take off on one foot.
- Take the ball on the way up.
- Catch the ball at the highest safest point (using the 'W' hand shape and forearms as shock absorbers).
- Counter-attack by throwing the ball quickly to the server

(8) Dealing with crosses with a supporting defender

Organisation

As in (7), but a defender is introduced. The purpose of this practice is to introduce communication and cooperation between the goalkeeper and his teammate.

Key points

- Adopt a good starting position (as in (7)).
- Take up a sideways stance.
- Instruct the defender where to stand.
- Assess the flight and pace of the ball.
- Decide whether to attack the ball or to stay.
- Communicate the decision – 'Keeper's!' or 'Away!'.
- If staying, get back to the line. If coming, take the ball at the highest safest point on the way up.
- Use the 'W' hand shape and the forearms as shock absorbers.

- If the goalkeeper comes to collect, the defender should drop to the line and provide cover.
- Counter-attack by throwing the ball quickly to the server.

(9) Dealing with crosses with two defenders and one attacker in attendance

Organisation

Similar to (8), but the keeper is assisted by two defenders and opposed by one attacker. As the goalkeeper gains in confidence more players can be added. Throughout the practice, the server crosses from wide positions with a variety of delivery angles. Occasionally he may set the ball back to a supporting player who crosses from a new position. This will force the keeper to push out the defenders and adjust his starting position. (See Figure 35.)

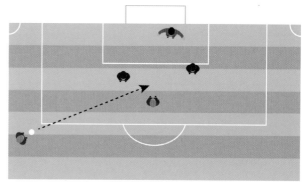

Figure 35 Dealing with crosses in a 2 v 2

Key points

- Adopt a good starting position (backwards from centre and off the line in relation to the position of the ball).
- Take up a sideways stance.
- Do not allow defenders to drop too deep unless the crosser is close to the goal line. Get them to hold a line.
- Assess the flight and pace of the ball.
- Decide whether to attack the ball or stay.
- Communicate the decision – 'Keeper's!' or 'Away!'
- If staying, move back to the line and prepare for a shot or header. If coming, take the ball at the highest safest point on the way up.

- Decide whether to catch, punch or deflect to safety.
- Apply the appropriate technique.
- The nearest defender should offer protection by occupying the space between the keeper and the attacker.
- The second defender should cover the line.

(10) Dealing with crosses delivered from a central area

Organisation
The service, which is kicked from the halfway line either side of the centre circle, is delivered between the penalty spot and the 6-yard box. Once the goalkeeper is comfortable dealing with the situation unopposed, a defender and opponent can be added as in practices (8) and (9).

Key points
- Adopt a starting position on the 6-yard line facing the ball.
- Assess the flight and pace of the ball.
- Take off on one foot.
- Take the ball on the way up.
- Catch the ball at the highest safest point (using the 'W' hand shape and forearms as shock absorbers).

(11) Dealing with crosses in a small-sided game

Organisation
The practice takes the form of a small-sided game (four against four with two wingers and two goalkeepers) in an area 40 × 60 yards. The players, who are not allowed past the halfway line, are arranged into two attackers versus two defenders in each half. The two wingers are 'floaters' who support the team in possession and are allowed to move unchallenged up and down a 5-yard channel.

The goalkeeper, or any one of the outfield players, passes the ball to the winger who makes ground before crossing into the opponent's goalmouth. Offsides apply. (See Figure 36.) Progress to introducing more players in each half.

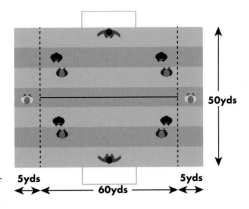

Figure 36 Crosses SSG

Key points
- Adopt a good starting position.
- Clear and early communication.
- Assessment of the flight and pace of the ball.
- Correct decision on whether to go or stay.
- Good technique.
- Defenders offer protection and cover the line.
- Good distribution.

HELPING THE BALL ON AND PUNCHING TECHNIQUES

(12) Helping on

Organisation
The goalkeeper sits on the ground while the server, from a distance of between 4 and 6 yards, throws the ball over the keeper's head. The keeper has to help the ball on to another server standing 3 yards behind. The service should almost be out of reach so that the keeper is unable to make a clean catch. (See photo 61.) Ensure that the service is delivered to both left and right hands.

Key points
- Assess the flight of the ball.
- Catch the ball if possible.
- If helping the ball on, use the fingers to alter its flight.
- Practise using the open and closed-hand techniques.

Photo 61 Helping on practice

(13) Turning the ball over the crossbar

Organisation

The goalkeeper positions himself ready for a cross. The server, standing at the junction of the 6-yard box and the goal line, throws the ball towards the crossbar.

Key points

- Adopt a good starting position.
- Take up a sideways stance.
- Assess the flight and pace of the ball.
- Decide whether to catch or deflect the ball over the bar.
- Turn the ball over the bar with the fingers using the open or closed-hand technique.

(14) Punching – one and two fisted

Organisation

The goalkeeper sits facing the server who feeds the ball from a distance of 2 or 3 yards to the keeper's right hand. He punches the ball back, aiming for the server's chest. The keeper punches 10 times with the right hand, 10 times with the left hand and 10 times with both.

Key points

- Keep the wrist rigid.
- Make contact with the flat part of the fist.
- Jab straight through the bottom half of the ball.
- Follow straight through.

(15) Punching from a lying position

Organisation

The keeper lies in the prone position facing the server, who positions himself a yard away. The server feeds the ball to the keeper's right hand and he punches the ball back. The goalkeeper looks to achieve height in the punch. Punch ten times with the right hand and then ten times with the left. (See photo 62.)

Key points

As in (14).

Photo 62 Punching from a lying position

(16) Punching off balance

Organisation

As in (14), but the direction and pace of service is varied and more challenging (including being bounced in and thrown well to the side). The keeper has to decide whether to use two fists or one. By varying the service the keeper will have to meet the challenge of ensuring that the ball and hand contact is correct. (See photo 63.)

Photo 63 Punching off balance

Key points
- Keep the wrists rigid.
- Make contact with the flat part of the wrist.
- Jab straight through the bottom half of the ball.
- Follow straight through.
- Be prepared to improvise with the heel of the hand if it is not possible to get the fist under the ball.

(17) Punching across the body

Organisation
The keeper kneels in the middle of a 6-yard goal facing outwards. A server standing 3 yards away throws the ball across the face of the goalkeeper who uses the nearest hand to punch the ball to a second server positioned at the other side of the goal. The action is then repeated from the other side so that the keeper works on both hands. Once the keeper has mastered the technique from the knees he should progress to the standing position and eventually to being put under pressure by an opponent.

Key points
- Keep the wrists rigid.
- Manipulate the wrist to ensure correct hand and ball contact.
- Use the pace and flight of the ball to achieve height, distance and width.

Dealing effectively with the low cross requires a combination of sound judgement and raw courage

The ball played in low and hard across the 6-yard box is a difficult one for the goalkeeper to deal with because there is usually a lack of time in which to assess the situation and there is the added pressure of any fumble being punished by a grateful opponent. To compound matters there are often other players in the vicinity and the keeper has to make a diving interception where the chances of being kicked are relatively high. However, these types of situations come with the territory, and it is the coach's responsibility to recreate match-like scenarios so that the goalkeeper develops good decision making backed up by the execution of the appropriate technique. As with the high cross, the keeper is faced with the choice of moving from the goal to intercept the ball (via a catch, punch, parry or deflection) or staying back to make a reaction save.

Usually with a low cross the crosser is closer to the goal, so the threat of a direct shot is greater than when the ball is in a wider position. This means that the keeper's starting position close to the near post has to cover the possibility of a shot or a cross. If the opponent shoots for goal the keeper has the full range of saving techniques at his disposal. On the other hand, if the ball is crossed and the keeper judges that it is within his range and elects to leave the goal line, he must be sure of at least clearing the immediate danger. Obviously a catch is the best solution but if this is not possible the ball should be punched, parried or deflected into safe areas.

In order to develop the keeper's proficiency in dealing with these situations, the coach should vary the crossing angle and distance to ensure that he faces in-swinging and out-swinging crosses. As with the high cross it is advisable to start with unopposed practices before introducing defenders and attackers.

(1) Dealing with the out-swinger

Organisation

A marker disc is placed at a 45 degree angle 20 yards from the right side near post. The crosser plays the ball past the marker with his right foot and, with his second touch, drives it towards the near post or across the 6-yard box (see Figure 37). When the keeper has mastered dealing with crosses from this position the coach can allow the crosser to have another touch so that the ball is delivered from close to the goal line. Another variation can involve changing the angle and distance of the cone. When the keeper is comfortable dealing with unopposed situations the coach can introduce one defender, then two defenders and one attacker and finally two defenders and two attackers.

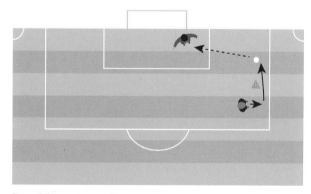

Figure 37 Low cross practice

Key points

- Adjust the starting position as the ball moves.
- Be set as the shot or cross is struck.
- Assess the pace and line of the ball.
- If dealing with a shot, choose the appropriate saving method.
- If dealing with a cross, decide whether to intercept or stay back.
- Communicate the decision to teammates.
- If staying back, retreat to the goal line to buy extra reaction time.
- If intercepting, get there first and decide whether to catch, punch, deflect or parry.
- Aim for high-quality technique.
- If necessary, rise quickly to make a secondary save.
- Consider the roles of fellow defenders to either mark players or space.

(2) Dealing with the in-swinger

Organisation

The set-up is the same as (1) above but the marker disc is placed on the left hand side of the goal. This time the crosser plays the ball away from the goal, past the cone and with the second touch whips the ball across the 6-yard box. The in-swinger presents the keeper with the danger of a shot at any time with the added complication of incoming players obscuring his view of the ball.

Key points

As in (1) above.

Balls played in behind the defence can cause havoc at all levels of the game yet it is the least practised of the goalkeeper's roles

When analysing goalkeeping activity during a game only a small percentage of the keeper's time is taken up by saving shots and dealing with crosses. Most of his work involves gamecraft – dealing with through balls, distribution and organising the defence. Unfortunately gamecraft is not given anywhere near the same amount of practice time that saving shots and taking crosses is. This is despite the indisputable fact that as the last line of the defensive unit, the goalkeeper is the team's safety net acting as a sweeper if the ball is played over his defence and as a passing option if his team cannot go forward. It is not realistic or fair to expect the young keeper to be a proficient reader of the game and a perceptive distributor of the ball, if little or no time is given to improving his gamecraft.

One of the most challenging gamecraft aspects to coach is dealing with through balls because it requires careful planning, sufficient space and access to the appropriate number of players. However, it must be addressed because quick thinking and astute positioning can diffuse potentially dangerous situations. On too many occasions a combination of a poor starting position, inaccurate assessment and an unsafe decision results in the keeper creating more problems than he solves.

In dealing with through balls there are four basic scenarios when the ball is played in behind the defence:

1 The ball reaches the penalty area and the keeper is able to collect it.

2 The ball lacks depth and the keeper has to leave the penalty area and play it with his feet.

3 Defenders are better placed to deal with the situation and the keeper prepares to receive a back pass.

4 An opponent is first to the ball and the keeper is faced with a 1 v 1 situation.

While these eventualities look easy to recognise, often during games the options are less clear cut. If goalkeeping was all about straightforward decisions it would be a much easier position, but unfortunately the game is more about shades of grey than black and white, and it is this lack of certainty that presents the keeper with the greatest challenge to his judgment.

Helping the goalkeeper to become a good reader of the game should be one of the coach's key objectives, and in terms of dealing with the through ball there are six key points to consider.

1 Distance from the goal line.

2 Distance from the rearmost defender.

3 Assessment.

4 Decision on the appropriate course of action.

5 Communicating the decision.

6 Taking positive action.

Distance from the goal line

The distance the goalkeeper should be from his own goal line varies according to the proximity of the ball. Obviously, his first priority is not to be beaten by a direct shot, but when the ball is some way from the goal, the keeper should maintain the optimum angle and distance so that he is ideally placed to intercept through balls and to support teammates who are in possession.

The following table and Figure 38 may be used as a guide:

Distance from the rearmost defender

All good defences are compact and the keeper should ensure that he does not become too detached from the rearmost defender. Skilful opponents will exploit large spaces left at the back of defences, so the goalkeeper should be aware of his sweeping role when the opposition is in possession.

Assessment

Having taken up a good supporting position, the keeper has to assess the scene in front of him and make a judgement on which of the four eventualities is about to happen.

Decision on the appropriate course of action

It is important that the goalkeeper chooses wisely because an impetuous rush from the penalty area could gift a goal to the opposition, or an ill-judged challenge could result in a free kick or penalty being awarded, followed by dismissal from the field of play. His decision will include one of the following:

• Wait until the ball reaches the area to collect it.
• Leave the area to play the ball with the feet.
• Allow teammates to make a clearance or execute a back pass.
• Prepare for a 1 v 1 situation.

Location of the ball	Keeper's distance from the goal line
In the opposition's penalty area.	18 yards
Between the opposition's penalty area and the halfway line.	12–18 yards
Between the halfway line and the arc of the centre circle.	6–10 yards
Between the arc of the centre circle and the edge of the penalty area.	3–6 yards

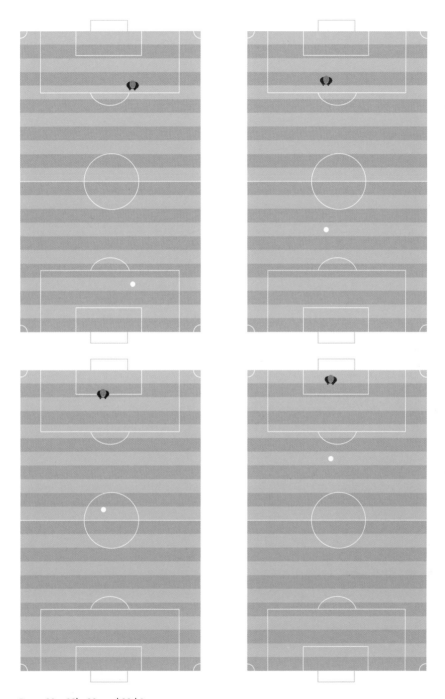

Figure 38a, 38b, 38c and 38d Supporting positions

Communicating the decision

Having made the decision, he should communicate his intentions to his fellow defenders. This information should be delivered early so teammates have time to react, loud so that his colleagues can hear and succinctly and unambiguously so that there is no confusion.

Positive action

Effective communication should be followed by positive action. The keeper cannot afford a moment's hesitation because there may be very little time available and dithering can hand the initiative to the opponent as well as creating confusion amongst his teammates. If he decides to meet the ball he must be the first to reach it and clear the immediate threat. If he elects to hold his ground he must prepare himself for a 1 v 1 situation or back pass. He must never get caught in two minds and leave himself in 'no man's land'. There will be occasions when he will make the wrong decision, but if his subsequent action is positive at least he will give his team a reasonable chance of averting the danger.

(1) Dealing with the through ball in a small-sided game

Organisation

This practice takes the form of 6 v 6 plus two goalkeepers in an area measuring 70 × 50 yards. The teams line up with two defenders, two midfielders and two strikers. The coach should set up the following scenarios to provide the keeper and his defence with realistic practice.

1   The goalkeeper's defence push up to the halfway line and one of the opposition's defenders plays a straight ball down the flank into the back of the defence.

2   The goalkeeper's centreback heads the ball weakly into the midfield area where it is played over his head into the space behind the defence.

3   The opposition midfield plays on to the feet of a striker who lays the ball off for a through ball into the back of the defence.

Key points
- Adopt a good starting position relative to the goal line and the ball.
- Keep in line with the ball.
- Stay compact with the rearmost defender.
- Assess the situation.
- Decide what course of action to take.
- Communicate the decision to teammates.
- Take positive action.

(2) Dealing with the through ball in an attack v defence phase of play

Organisation

This practice takes place in one half of the field where there is an 8 v 8 plus one goalkeeper situation. The opponents' back and midfield players are conditioned to playing the ball behind the defence while the goalkeeper's team have to run the ball through one of two targets 10 yards into the opposing half either side of the centre circle to register a goal. (See Figure 39.)

Key points

- Adopt a good starting position.
- Stay compact with the rearmost defender.
- Support teammates when they are in possession.
- Impart high quality information.
- Make good decisions.
- Take positive action.
- Inspire colleagues with confidence.

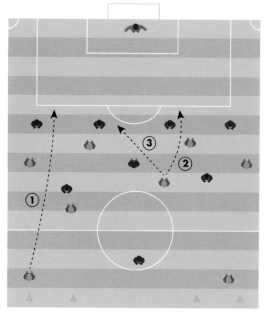

Figure 39 Through balls in an attack v defence phase of play

If the goalkeeper is the last line of defence he is, by implication, the first line of attack, and in the modern game he has to be one of the most proficient passers of the ball in the team

It is essential that the coach works on perfecting his keeper's throwing and passing techniques from an early age as the young keeper will have many opportunities to distribute the ball during any given game. Obviously expectations will be largely determined by the goalkeeper's age and physique. For example, it would be unrealistic for an 8-year-old to master the javelin throw or the wedge pass because they are simply not physically capable. Nevertheless coaches who neglect working on distribution from the keeper do so at their own peril.

The goalkeeper should constantly practise throwing and kicking techniques so that his distribution becomes an asset rather than a liability to the team. Since he has to take more free kicks (for offsides and goal kicks mostly) than any other player, it is essential that he is one of the most proficient dead-ball kickers in the team. In addition to being able to kick the ball over long distances the keeper must have a range of consistently accurate passing techniques. If he is reliable with his kicks, the team can

then adapt their tactics accordingly. However, if a goalkeeper's distribution is erratic, his kicking will take on a negative rather than a positive connotation.

THROWING TECHNIQUES

The roll

The roll is used for very short distances, usually to pass to defenders on the edge of the penalty area. The actual technique is similar to the ten pin bowling action where the ball is kept in contact with the ground for as long as possible. The keeper can achieve this by bending the knees and following through on the roll. (See photos 64a, 64b, 64c and 64d.)

Photo 64a, 64b, 64c, 64d The roll

The javelin

This is used for slightly longer distances and involves a whiplash action which resembles throwing a javelin. By flicking the wrist on delivery, slice will be bestowed on the ball, thus keeping the bounce low. The risk of giving the receiver a difficult bouncing ball will be further reduced if the keeper stays low throughout the delivery. Ideally, the ball should reach the recipient below knee height. (See photo 65.) As with the roll the leading foot points in the direction of the intended target while the back one is square on to the direction of travel.

Photo 65 The javelin   Photo 66 The sling

The sling

The sling can be used as an alternative to the javelin throw and is used for medium distances. For younger goalies with small hands this technique is easier to learn than the javelin. Here the keeper takes a wider stance where bending the knees can help keep the ball low. The ball is taken back with a straight side arm and then is swept across the body at which point it is released. (See photo 66.)

The overarm

If performed well and employed at the appropriate moment, this throw can be a potent attacking weapon because it can play several opponents out of the game at one time. It is used to cover distances beyond which the keeper would have to kick. It is often employed when the opposition have committed numbers in attack and the goalkeeper tries to catch them on the break. These throws are more effective when kept low because they take less time to reach their intended target. However, when opponents are blocking the direct route, the ball has to spend most of its journey airborne.

The actual technique is similar to a cricket bowling action where the goalkeeper takes the ball back with a fairly straight arm and follows through quite vigorously brushing the ear on the way. Raising the opposite hand will ensure that the head is kept steady and assist accuracy. The point of release depends on how much air the keeper intends to give the ball. If he is looking to clear players, then an early release is recommended, but if there are no obstacles between himself and his target, not only can he release the ball late, but he can also impart slice in order to keep it low. The front foot should be pointed in the direction of travel while the back foot is planted square to the target. (See photo sequence 67.)

Photo sequence 67 The overarm throw

KICKING TECHNIQUES FROM THE GROUND

Approximately 60–70 per cent of a goalkeeper's work at the highest level is undertaken with the feet so it is essential that he develops a range of proficient kicking techniques from an early age. There are four kicking techniques from the ground and three from the hands.

The side foot

Used for short distances up to 20 yards this pass is played with a stiff side foot and the contact is made through the mid-centre of the ball. The non-kicking foot is placed alongside the ball. As a general rule it is better to overhit than underhit short passes to reduce the chances of interception.

The drill

Used for distances of 20–40 yards, contact is made through the mid-centre of the ball with the instep. Locking the ankle and keeping the knee over the ball will ensure that it is kept low and presents few control problems for the recipient. The non-kicking foot is placed alongside the ball. (See Photo 68.)

The wedge

Used to bypass players over a distance of 20–40 yards, contact is made through the bottom middle of the ball with the instep. The objective is to play the ball through the air so that it arrives on the recipient's thigh or chest. With the body slightly leaning back, the non-kicking foot is placed to the side and ahead of the ball. Care must be taken not to overhit the pass. (See Photo 69.)

The drive

Used for long distances such as playing the ball into the opponent's half, contact is made with the instep through the bottom middle of the ball to achieve elevation. Placing the non-kicking foot to the side and in front of the ball and leading with the front shoulder will help to reduce the chances of slicing the delivery. After contact there should be a long smooth follow-through. (See photos 70a and 70b.)

Goal kick strategies

Goalkeepers who consistently achieve distance and accuracy from their dead-ball kicks will prove an asset to the team. It is demoralising for a team to be regularly put on the defensive by a keeper's weak kicking. However, even though he fails to clear any great distance, the keeper can save the day if he can kick accurately to strategically placed teammates. The coach should be aware of his goalkeeper's strengths and weaknesses in this department and should implement an appropriate pattern of play. If the keeper consistently kicks long, he can push players well forward into the opponent's half since players cannot be offside from a goal kick. But, if the keeper repeatedly fails to reach the halfway line, the target players can drop deeper in order to win the first touch.

Coaches of school and youth teams should persevere with their goalkeepers even if their goal kicks are poor. Players at this level are at a crucial stage of their development and should not be denied learning experiences such as taking goal kicks. If the keeper is not permitted to take his own goal kicks there will be little motivation

Photo 68 The drill

Photo 69 The wedge

Photo 70a and 70b The drive

for him to improve his technique. Moreover, having an outfield player taking goal kicks encourages the opposing strikers to push forwards in the knowledge that they will not be offside if the ball is returned by their midfield or defence.

If the coach is concerned about the lack of distance achieved by his young keeper's kicks, he should strategically place defenders in the penalty area so that opponents gaining possession are immediately put under pressure. According to the laws of the game, opponents must take up positions outside the penalty area, whereas the team taking the goal kick can go where they please.

KICKING TECHNIQUES FROM THE HANDS

The volley

The volley is the most common method used when kicking from the hands. The advantages of the volley are that the ball can be passed over considerable distances and it is fairly reliable. With the volley and half-volley techniques the keeper should drop rather than toss up the ball before striking it. The longer the ball is in the air, especially in windy conditions, the greater the chances of a poor kick. By almost placing the ball on to the foot the goalkeeper can improve the quality of the contact and, in turn, increase the reliability of his kicks (See photos 71 sequence.)

The half-volley

If executed well, the half-volley is a more effective technique than the volley because its lower trajectory results in the ball reaching its target in a shorter time. It is useful when playing into a strong wind or when there is an opportunity for a quick counter-attack. However, care must be taken when playing on muddy or bumpy grounds because good contact with the ball cannot be guaranteed. With this in mind it is not recommended to attempt this technique in the 6-yard area. (See photo 72 sequence.)

Photo 71 sequence The volley

Photo 72 sequence The half-volley

The hook volley

The main benefit of the hook volley is that it can give the ball a fairly flat trajectory and can reach the target quickly without creating major control problems. It is therefore a good counter-attacking weapon. The ball is presented on to the kicking foot with the opposite hand where it is volleyed from outside the line of the body using the instep. (See photo 73 sequence.)

(2) The roll to a moving target

Organisation

As in (1), but on the command the receiver sets off at an angle and the keeper has to find him with a rolled pass.

Photo 73 sequence The hook volley

The dribble and drive

If it is safe to do so, the goalkeeper may elect to drop the ball and, rather than clear from the hands, dribble with it before kicking from the ground. Kicking from the ground is not advisable when opponents are nearby or if conditions are heavy, and it is not easy to achieve elevation on the ball. Care should be taken to place the ball at the two o' clock position for right footed kicks and ten o' clock for left footed kicks.

(1) The roll to stationary target

Organisation

The keeper rolls the ball to a receiver standing 6–10 yards away. The receiver controls and then returns the ball.

Key points

- Point the leading foot in the direction of the target.
- Use a ten pin bowling action.
- Keep low by bending the front knee.
- Ensure a good follow-through.
- Do not give the receiver control problems – keep the ball low.

Key points

- As in (1) but aim slightly in front of the receiver so that he does not have to check his stride.

(3) The javelin throw to a stationary target

Organisation

The keeper uses the javelin throw to pass to a receiver standing 10–15 yards away. The receiver controls and then returns the ball.

Key points

- Point the front foot and non-throwing arm in the direction of the target.
- Keep low with the back foot square to the target.
- Use a javelin arm action.
- Flick the wrist on delivery to impart slice on the ball.
- Keep the ball low so that the receiver does not have a control problem.

(4) The javelin throw to a moving target

Organisation

As for (3), but on the command the receiver sets off at an angle and the keeper has to pass to him using a javelin throw.

Key points

- As in (3) but aim slightly in front of the receiver so that he does not have to check his stride.

(5) The sling to a stationary target

Organisation

The keeper uses the sling to pass to a receiver standing 15–25 yards away. The receiver controls and then returns the ball.

Key points

- Point the front foot and non-throwing arm in the direction of the target.
- Bend the front knee and ensure that the back foot is planted.
- Take the ball back with a straight side arm.
- Sweep the arm through quickly (as if cutting corn) and release.
- Keep the ball low so that the receiver does not have a control problem.

(6) The sling to a moving target

Organisation

As for (5), but on the command the receiver sets off at an angle and the keeper has to pass to him using the sling.

Key points

- As in (5) but aim slightly in front of the receiver so that he does not have to check his stride.

(7) The overarm throw to a stationary target

Organisation

The keeper throws the ball using the overarm technique to a target 15–35 yards away. The receiver controls and then returns the ball.

Key points

- Point the leading foot and non-throwing arm towards the target.
- Place the back foot square to the target.
- Ensure a straight arm preparation.
- Use a fast follow-through and a late release.
- Flick the fingers on delivery to impart slice on the ball.
- Keep the ball low so that the receiver is not presented with a control problem.

(8) The overarm throw – clearing an opponent

Organisation

As for (7), but an opponent stands in the line of flight so that the keeper has to clear him to find his target.

Key points

- Point the leading foot and non-throwing arm towards the target.
- Place the back foot square to the target.
- Ensure a straight arm preparation.
- Use a slow follow-through with an early release.
- Aim to drop the ball at the receiver's feet.

(9) The overarm throw to a moving target

Organisation

As for (7), but on the command the receiver sets off at an angle and the keeper has to find him using an overarm throw.

Key points

- As in (7) but aim slightly in front of the receiver so that he does not have to check his stride.

(10) The overarm throw to a moving target – clearing an opponent

Organisation
As for (8), but the receiver sets off at an angle and the keeper has to clear the opponent to find his teammate.

Key points
• As in (8) but aim to drop the ball at the receiver's feet so that he does not have to check his stride.

(11) Choosing the correct throwing method and using the correct technique

Organisation
The server plays the ball into the goalkeeper's hands who, having caught the ball, throws to a target player positioned at varying angles and distances from the goal. The keeper has to assess the distance and use the appropriate throwing technique. Progress from throwing to a stationary target to distributing to a moving target. (See Figure 40.)

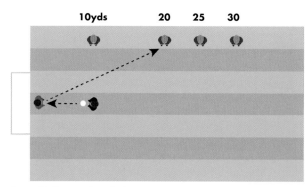

Figure 40 Choosing the right throwing option

Key points
• Catch the ball safely without bringing it into the chest.
• Scan the target while moving forwards.
• Assess the distance.
• Choose the appropriate throwing method.
• Aim for the receiver's back foot.

(12) The side foot pass

Organisation
The ball is played into the keeper from 10 yards. The keeper uses his first touch to control the ball out of his feet before passing back to the server with the second. Progress to controlling with one foot and passing back with the other.

Key points
• Move in to line with the ball.
• Use the inside of the foot to control the ball.
• Play the ball out of the feet (two o'clock if passing with the right foot, ten o'clock if passing with the left foot).
• Place the non-kicking foot alongside the ball.
• Contact through the mid-centre of the ball.
• Keep the ankle stiff.
• Ensure that the pass is accurate and well weighted.

(13) The drill pass

Organisation
This practice, which recreates a switch move, takes place in the goalmouth, where the keeper receives a pass from his right back standing 25–30 yards away. The keeper controls the ball out of his feet in the direction of travel and drills the ball out to his left back 25–30 yards away. Aim to play the ball slightly in front of the receiver. (See Figure 41.)

Key points
• Using the inside of the foot control the ball out of the feet with the first touch (two o'clock or ten o'clock).
• Check the location of the target.
• Place the non-kicking foot alongside the ball.
• Using the instep strike through the mid-centre of the ball.
• Lock the ankle and keep the knee over the ball.
• Ensure that the pass is accurate and well weighted.

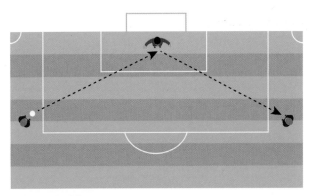

Figure 41 The drill practice

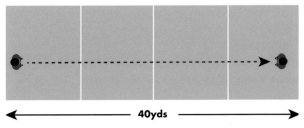

Figure 42 The drive practice

(14) The wedge pass

Organisation

The server passes to the keeper who plays the first touch out of the feet before lofting the ball to a target player 30–35 yards away at various angles.

Key points

- Using the inside of the foot control the ball out of the feet with the first touch (two o' clock or ten o' clock).
- Check the location of the target.
- Place the non-kicking foot alongside and in front of the ball.
- Using the instep, strike through the bottom centre of the ball.
- Lean back and follow through after contact.
- Do not overhit and aim for the recipient's thigh or chest.

(15) The drive

Organisation

The keeper kicks the ball over four 10-yard grids to a target player. (See Figure 42.) As the goalkeeper becomes proficient, extend the target range by one set of grids so that the keeper is kicking over 50 yards. If two goalkeepers are working at the same task a competition could by organised with the winner being the first to complete ten successful kicks. To achieve a successful kick the ball has to reach the target without bouncing.

Key points

- Check the location of the target.
- Make an angled approach – two o'clock position for a right-footed kick, ten o'clock position for a left-footed kick.
- The non-kicking foot should be positioned to the side and in front of the ball.
- The kicking foot should be pointed outwards, with the ankle firm and extended.
- Contact should be made with the instep through the bottom half of the ball.
- The eyes should be looking down at the ball with the head steady.
- Ensure a long smooth follow-through.
- Relax, don't try too hard.

When kicking against a strong wind, the keeper should aim for a lower trajectory by reducing the run-up and the angle of approach, and also by planting the non-kicking foot closer to the ball.

(16) Dribble and drive

Organisation

As for (15), but this time the goalkeeper drops the ball, plays the ball out of the feet, and kicks it to the target standing 40–50 yards away. Vary the distance to suit the needs of the players. Make it competitive – the winner is the first to perform ten successful kicks.

Key points

- Roll the ball out of the feet to the two o'clock position if right-footed or the ten o'clock position if left-footed.
- Check the location of the intended target.
- Ensure that the position of the ball allows a reasonable run-up.
- The non-kicking foot should be positioned to the side and in front of the ball.
- The kicking foot should be pointed outwards, with the ankle firm and extended.
- Contact should be made with the instep through the bottom half of the ball.
- Ensure a relaxed and smooth follow-through.
- The eyes should be looking down at the ball, with the head steady.

(17) The volley

Organisation
As for (15). Vary the distance to suit the needs of the players.

Key points

- Hold the ball with two hands out in front of the body at waist height.
- Check the location of the intended target.
- Drop the ball on to the kicking foot.
- Using the instep (laces), strike the ball in front of the body.
- Place the non-kicking foot behind the line of the ball.
- Make contact through the middle of the ball.
- Ensure a smooth follow-through.
- Keep the head steady, with the eyes fixed on the ball.
- Relax, do not try too hard.

(18) The half-volley

Organisation
As for (17) but the goalkeeper half-volleys the ball to the receiver.

Key points
- Check the location of the intended target.
- Hold the ball in two hands in front of the body at waist height.
- Drop the ball so that it pitches just in front of the non-kicking foot.
- Use the instep of the kicking foot, striking through the bottom half of the ball just as it hits the ground.
- Ensure a smooth follow-through, with the body leaning backwards.
- Keep the head steady, with the eyes fixed on the ball.
- Relax, do not try too hard.

To achieve a lower trajectory, the ball should be dropped closer to the non-kicking foot and contact should be made through the centre of the ball. The knee should be over the ball, with the body leaning forwards on the follow-through.

(19) The hook volley

Organisation
As for (17) and (18), but the goalkeeper hook volleys the ball to the receiver

Key points
- Check the location of the intended target.
- Using the opposite hand present the ball at waist height outside the line of the body.
- Angle the instep to hit through the middle of the ball to control the trajectory.
- To keep the ball lower, hit down into the ball.
- Lean back on contact.
- Use the follow-through to control the pace on the ball – a fast long follow through will make the ball go quicker.

(20) Kicking to a variety of targets

Organisation
The practice takes place on the pitch with a range of targets placed around the halfway line. Vary the distance to suit the ability of the players. So that progress can be monitored, points are awarded for accurate kicks. The keeper should practise all three kicking methods.

Key points
As for (17), (18) and (19).

DISTRIBUTION
BUILDING FROM THE BACK AND COUNTER-ATTACKING

No-one initiates more attacks than the goalkeeper

Since the goalkeeper has possession of the ball more than any other player, it is imperative that he uses it well. It is infuriating to see a keeper having made a fine catch, surrender possession through a careless throw or kick. Indeed often at the moment the keeper makes a save, the opposition is at its most vulnerable in terms of a counter-attack. With six seconds and the whole of the penalty area at his disposal, speedy and incisive distribution can have devastating results.

The manner in which the head coach instructs his goalkeeper to distribute the ball will form the basis for the team's pattern of play. Some coaches who prefer to build up from the back will encourage their goalkeeper to throw or play the ball short at every opportunity so that possession can be retained. Others will prefer their keepers to miss out the defence and midfield by kicking deep into enemy territory in order to maximise his own team's strengths and/or to exploit the weaknesses of his opponents.

Throws are generally quicker and more accurate than kicks so the keeper should learn to use them to good effect. It is important, therefore, that a ball thrown by the goalkeeper does not give the recipient a control problem. If the recipient has to waste precious seconds in controlling the ball, it defeats the whole object of the exercise. The throw or pass should also set the receiver up for his next touch. If the teammate has half-turned it may be possible to play the ball to his back foot (the one closest to the opponent's goal) so that he can make progress up the pitch. On the other hand, if the recipient does not have space in front of him the ball should be played to his front (or safe) foot.

Having mastered the techniques of throwing and kicking, the keeper must develop an understanding of when and where to use them. When counter-attacking, as soon as the goalkeeper collects the ball he must move forward quickly holding the ball in front of him primed and ready for a throw or kick. When moving forward the goalkeeper should be scanning the whole pitch looking for the opportunity to exploit where the opposition is weak defensively. Counter-attacking is all about speed of thought, movement and ball.

The good goalkeeper will quickly assess the situation and identify the following:

- Areas where the opposition's defensive arrangement is vulnerable (for example no covering defenders at the back of the defence).

- His teammates' strengths (for example his most forward player may have great pace and would benefit from a ball hit behind the opposition's defence).

- The options available to him (for example switching play to the opposite flank with a fast throw into space).

- The most appropriate method of distribution.

On a cautionary note, however, the goalkeeper should not be thinking about the throw before making the save. Many keepers have been embarrassed because they have taken their eye off the ball at the last minute.

The goalkeeper's distribution should not put his own goal under immediate threat. An understanding of risk assessment will help the keeper to make sensible selections. With a wayward kick into the opponent's half, his team has half of the field to regain possession, whereas a risky short throw or pass to a teammate can spell disaster. He must not pass the ball to colleagues in his own half when there is little chance of their retaining possession.

Sometimes the state of play will dictate how the keeper distributes. If his team is under severe pressure, the goalkeeper is advised to take the heat out of the situation by placing the ball on the ground and executing a dribble and drive. Of course, this can only be attempted when there are no opponents in the vicinity. He should also be able to assess the strengths and weaknesses of the opposition and distribute the ball accordingly. For instance, it would be futile persisting with high clearances when his own forwards are dwarfed by the opposing defenders. As all opponents are different and pose varying problems and challenges, it is important that teams demonstrate tactical flexibility, which of course includes a range of distribution options from the goalkeeper.

(1) When and how 1

Organisation

This practice is about making the correct decisions and applying the appropriate technique in that it is designed to help the goalkeeper to select the best distribution option and to execute it effectively. The ball is played into the goal area where the keeper collects (see Figure 43). He then runs forward and has to choose from one of three targets at varying distances from the goal. The coach moves to block off the passing lane to one of the targets. The object of the exercise is to choose the most penetrative option and to execute the most effective form of distribution with appropriate quality. The coach assesses the goalkeeper on three areas (i) correct decision (ii) most appropriate distribution method (iii) quality of distribution. The same organisation can be used for distribution from the hands and feet.

Key points

- After collecting, move forward scanning the options.
- Choose the most penetrative unmarked option.
- Choose the appropriate distribution method.
- Choose to pass to feet or space.
- Ensure quality distribution.

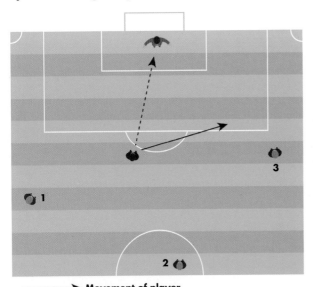

—————▶ **Movement of player**
- - - - -▶ **Movement of ball**

Figure 43 When and how 1

(2) When and how 2

Organisation

This practice takes place in one half of the field with six defenders versus four attackers. When the attackers win the ball they must play into the goalkeeper who now looks for a counter-attacking opportunity. Given that the keeper's team has a numerical superiority at least one of his teammates will be free. They then score a 'goal' by running the ball through one of two gates on the halfway line. (See Figure 44.)

Key points

As in (1) above.

(3) When and how small-sided game

Organisation

This practice takes place on a pitch 60 × 40 yards and involves two goalkeepers, 5 v 5 and two floating players supporting the team in position. Whenever the goalkeeper takes possession of the ball, two players should be free which should make his decisions on counter-attacking more straightforward. As the goalkeeper's understanding improves remove one of the floating players.

Key points

As in (1) above.

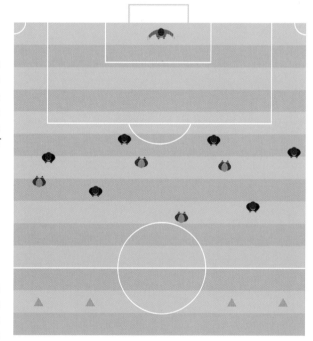

Figure 44 When and how 2

Goalkeepers who are not comfortable with the back pass are a liability to their team

The law that a keeper may not use his hands if receiving the ball from a back pass means that the keeper has to be as comfortable with the ball at his feet as he is with it in his hands. This entails demonstrating good ball control as well as being proficient with both feet for long and short passes. Consequently, it is crucial that sufficient time is set aside to master and then polish these techniques. Warm-ups and cool-downs present the ideal times for this type of practice. Despite the back pass occurring frequently during matches, it is rarely specifically practised as part of squad training. This is an alarming oversight.

Players pass the ball back to their goalkeeper for the following reasons:

- As an emergency measure when they have nowhere else to go.

- They cannot pass forward themselves.

- To 'buy' the team some time.

- To provide a point through which the team can switch the direction of play.

- To maintain possession of the ball.

This means that the goalkeeper will not only have to make effective clearances under pressure, but also display the composure to control and pass the ball accurately when time and space is available.

One principle should dominate the goalkeeper's approach to dealing with back passes – safety. Since he is the last line of defence, he cannot afford to take risks, because one error of judgement can spell disaster. For this reason, he should avoid taking more touches than necessary and he should never attempt to dribble round an opponent. Memories of needlessly conceded goals because of a reckless attitude will haunt the goalkeeper for a long time. Instead, the keeper should follow the age old maxim, 'if in doubt put it out'. Dealing with the back pass involves two stages – preparation and distribution.

PREPARATION

Assessment

As play develops towards him the keeper has to identify that a back pass is a possibility and adopt an appropriate supporting position.

Distance of support

The goalkeeper must leave sufficient space for his teammate to pass the ball to him. If he takes up a position too close to his colleague he will put unnecessary pressure on the pass and also leave himself little time to deal with it once it arrives. In preparing to receive a back pass, the goalkeeper should take up a position that provides the passer with some margin of error. A pressurised colleague would rather pass over ten yards than one or two, so the goalkeeper must retreat to make the passing distance more appealing.

Angle of support

As the keeper's primary task is to protect the goal he should not take up a position that leaves it wide open. It is recommended that he positions himself between the ball and the goal so that if his

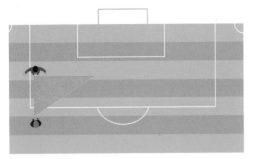

Figure 45 Angle and distance of back pass: incorrect supporting position

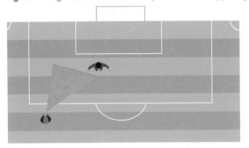

Figure 46 Angle and distance of back pass: correct supporting position

teammate misdirects the back pass it does not result in disastrous consequences. If the back pass is wayward, let it be at the expense of a corner and not an own goal. (See Figures 45 and 46.)

Communication

An early call will help his teammate decide that the back pass is the best option. Furthermore the intonation of his voice should convey the urgency of the situation. For example, if his teammate is under severe pressure the keeper should shout 'Man on! Pass it back early!' in an excited manner. On the other hand, when his colleague is under minimal pressure his call should be calm and indicate that the situation is not an emergency.

DISTRIBUTION

Time available

The proximity of the nearest opponent will indicate to the goalkeeper how many touches he can safely take. Needless to say if the opponent is very close then the clearance should be made with one touch. If pressure on the ball is insignificant, then the keeper will have the time to control the ball before making an accurate pass.

Direction of the pass

The opponent's angle of approach will dictate where the keeper should play the pass. If the keeper clears too close to the opponent the ball may rebound off him into the empty net. For this reason the pass should be angled away from the opponent's line of approach. If taking more than one touch, the keeper's first touch should take him away from the opponent.

Type of pass

If the goalkeeper has sufficient time he should choose how he will control the ball – with which part of the foot or other controlling surface – relax on contact, play the ball out of his feet and then make the pass. However, if time and space are at a premium, he will have to make a first-time clearance. Often the surfaces of goal areas are uneven and the keeper must take care that a good contact is made with the ball. Height and distance on the clearance will provide time for the defence to recover, so the keeper must concentrate on striking through the bottom half of the ball. This is fairly easy to achieve when the ball comes from the side but when the back pass is made straight at the keeper's feet with very little room for a reasonable back-lift, he should use the side of the foot to lift the ball over the first line of opponents.

When passing over short distances, for example to the nearest full back, the keeper should overhit rather than underhit the pass. If the pass has insufficient weight it increases the possibility of an interception. On the other hand, if the pass is too strong for the full back the worst that can happen is a throw-in conceded.

In order to cope with the full range of eventualities, the keeper should work on a range of unopposed and game-related activities aimed at developing technical proficiency with both feet.

His fellow defenders should also work with him to develop an understanding of relative strengths and weaknesses. If the back pass is made to the keeper's weaker foot or if he is under severe pressure, the team should concentrate on damage limitation and move in field to become more compact. This assumes that possession will be lost and the team should prepare to defend. However, if the pass is made to the goalkeeper's stronger foot and he is under little pressure, the team should spread out and attempt to build an attack.

(1) Two-touch passing

Organisation
The keeper stands in a grid measuring 2 × 2 yards. From a distance of 10–15 yards the server plays the ball to the keeper who has to control the ball with one touch out of the square and pass back to the server (see Figure 47). Progress to controlling with one foot and passing with the other.

Key points
- Get into line.
- Control the ball out of the feet, two o'clock for the right foot and ten o'clock for the left foot.
- Firm accurate pass back to the server.

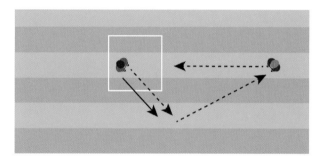

Figure 47 Two touch passing

(2) One- or two-touch passing

Organisation
From a distance of 10–15 yards the server plays the ball at various heights and speeds to the goalkeeper. As he releases the ball the server shouts 'One!' or 'Two!' and the keeper has to respond using the appropriate number of touches.

Key points
- Get into line.
- If two touches, select controlling surface.
- If one touch, ensure firm contact with foot or head.
- Relax on contact to play the ball out of the feet.
- Ensure a good quality pass on the second touch.

(3) Keep ball

Organisation
This practice takes place in a square 15 × 15 yards with a goalkeeper on each side. With a defender in the middle, the keepers on the outside have to keep possession without using their hands. Change the defender after every two minutes.

Key points
- Provide a passing angle for the man in possession.
- As the ball is on its way, quickly get into line.
- Decide on the number of touches to take.
- Control and pass away from the defender.

(4) Switching play

Organisation
Using the full width of the pitch, server 1, standing in the right back position, plays the ball to the goalkeeper who has to control across the body and pass to server 2 standing in the left back position. (See Figure 48.) Progress to server 3 putting pressure on the keeper so he has to decide on the number of touches and the direction of his pass.

Key points
- Take up a good supporting position.
- Adopt an open body position when receiving the ball.
- Be aware of the proximity of the nearest closing player.
- Control across the body.
- Pass accurately (using the drill technique) into the teammate's path.
- Overhit rather than underhit.

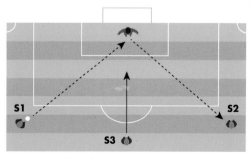

Figure 48 Switching play

(5) 2 v 1 game

Organisation

This practice is designed to test the keeper's composure under pressure. In an area measuring 20 × 20 yards, two outfield players exchange passes. Without warning, the ball is passed back to the goalkeeper. The passer then puts the goalkeeper under pressure while the other player makes an angle to receive the pass. (See Figure 49.)

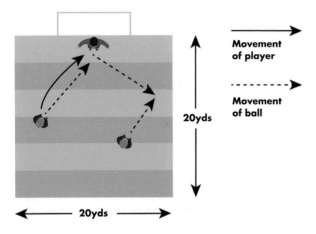

Figure 49 2 v 1 game

Key points

- Get into line.
- Assess the proximity and the angle of approach of the opponent.
- Decide on the number of touches available.
- Control and pass away from the opponent.
- Teammate should make a good passing angle.
- Support the pass.
- Do not take risks.

(6) Long clearances

Organisation

This practice aims to help the goalkeeper to improve his ability to play long after receiving a back pass. The practice takes place over 40 × 10 yard grid with the keeper at one end and a target player (T) at the other (see Figure 50). The server (S) passes the ball to the keeper, who has to clear the server and reach the target. The server varies his position and occasionally pressurises the pass so that the keeper has to clear first time.

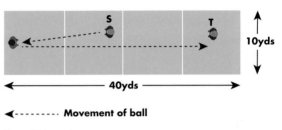

◄- - - - - - - - **Movement of ball**

Figure 50 Long clearances

Key points

- Get into line.
- Decide upon the appropriate number of touches.
- If two touch, control out of the feet.
- Aim for height to clear the pressurising player.
- Do not take risks.

(7) Long or short

Organisation

The practice is designed to assist the keeper in his decision making on whether to play long or short. It takes place over a 40 × 15 yard area with the goalkeeper in the end grid (see Figure 51). Server 1 plays the ball into the keeper at which point server 2 pressurises the pass. The keeper has to choose whether to play short to server 1, who has taken a supporting position, or long to the target player (T).

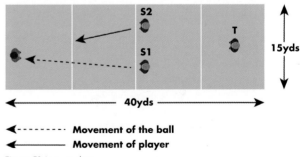

◄- - - - - - - - **Movement of the ball**
◄———————— **Movement of player**

Figure 51 Long or short

Key points

- Get into line.
- Access the proximity and angle of approach of pressurising player.
- Decide on appropriate number of touches.
- Decide on the target.
- If playing short, overhit rather than underhit.
- If playing long aim for height to clear pressurising player.

(8) Back pass under varying degrees of pressure

Organisation

The coach controls the service in this practice to meet the needs of his keeper. The practice takes place in the defensive half of the field with the coach serving the ball from the edge of the penalty area. On the coach's command an opponent pressurises the goalkeeper, who has to find one of two target players spread across the field. (See Figure 52.) The coach tests the goalkeeper's ability to deal with the pass by varying the service and the degree of pressure.

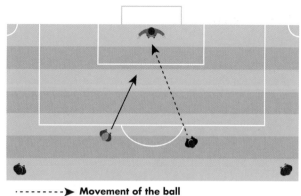

- - - - - - ▷ **Movement of the ball**
——————▶ **Movement of player**

Figure 52 Back pass under varying degrees of pressure

Key points

- Get into line.
- Assess the proximity and the angle of approach of the opponent.
- Decide on the number of touches available.
- If one touch, ensure good contact on the clearance. If more than one touch, control and pass away from the opponent.
- If passing long, aim for height and distance.
- Teammates should make good passing angles.
- If appropriate, support the pass.
- Do not take risks.

(9) The back pass small-sided game

Organisation

This practice takes place in an area of 60 × 40 yards in a 7 v 7 game. If the team regains possession in its own half it must pass back to the goalkeeper before the ball can cross the halfway line. The aims of the game are to practise dealing with the back pass under realistic conditions, and to develop an understanding with fellow defenders.

Key points

As for (8)

ORGANISING THE DEFENCE
COMMUNICATION

The good goalkeeper controls their defence like a conductor directs an orchestra

As the last line of the defence, the goalkeeper should use his excellent view of the whole field to direct defensive operations like the conductor of an orchestra. Whereas the conductor communicates with his baton, the goalkeeper uses his voice.

Goalkeepers who communicate well with fellow defenders are greatly valued. Clear, precise, early calls can alert teammates to hitherto unforeseen dangers as well as averting any confusion. Also, constant pertinent communication with his defenders will aid the keeper's concentration, especially during those periods in the game when he is largely inactive.

Effective communication is what is heard rather than what is said and I get a little frustrated with people who exhort their young goalies to 'talk' to the defence without a real understanding of what should be said. If the keeper just chunters on endlessly without much of the content being relevant or helpful, his teammates will just switch off. I often hear goalkeepers being vocal when play is some distance from the goal but when the ball is in and around the penalty area they suddenly go quiet, ironically at a time when his defenders most need direction. Developing good communication skills comes with experience, confidence and a growing understanding of the roles of his fellow defenders. So to expect young keepers to be proficient organisers of the defence is simply unrealistic.

When

The timing of the communication is critical. The calls must be early enough for his teammates to respond appropriately. Acting as the team's early warning system, the keeper can nip potential danger in the bud by providing vital information. Whether it is a fairly straightforward call when advancing for a through ball, or a subtle adjustment to the shape of the defensive unit, it must be early. Late calls, when teammates are already committed

There are three elements to communication:

1 TIMING (WHEN) – early so that teammates have time to respond.

2 CONTENT (WHAT) – specific, succinct and relevant.

3 DELIVERY (HOW) – loud, clear and with authority.

to a course of action, can cause considerable confusion and significantly reduce the team's confidence in their keeper.

What

It is important that the goalkeeper knows what to communicate. He should be fully conversant with his team's defensive strategy so that he can ensure that his teammates adhere to the agreed tactics, both for set pieces and free play. He should not only be able to alert defenders to the movement of opponents, but also to provide useful information when his team has possession. An understanding of the individual roles of his teammates both in and out of possession will help in this regard.

The vocabulary used by the keeper should be easily understood by his teammates so that they can take the appropriate action. Communication should be short and unambiguous as precious seconds can be wasted by instructions that are long-winded and confusion caused by vague directions. The coach can help the young goalkeeper by providing a vocabulary list of commonly used instructions.

WHEN IN POSSESSION

When the teammate has time on the ball:

'Time – two-touch!'

'Time, turn!'

'Time, take it away!'

When the teammate has time and should switch play:

'Time, switch it!'

When the teammate is under pressure:

'Man on!'

'Away, man on!'

'Play it safe, man on!'

When the keeper wants the ball-carrier to pass the ball back:

'Keeper's on, push it back!'

'Keeper's on, head it back!'

When the keeper wants the player to leave the through ball:

'Keeper's let it run/go!'

WHEN NOT IN POSSESSION

When the keeper wants the teammate to pressurise the ball carrier:

'Get tighter!'

'Close him down quickly!'

'Stay on your feet!'

When the keeper wants to make play predictable:

'Don't let him turn!'

'Show him inside/down the line!'

When the ball has been cleared and he wants the defence to make play compact:

'Step up!' (If done gradually.)

'Squeeze!' (If done quickly over a reasonable distance.)

When the keeper wants the defence to hold a line:

'Hold the edge!' (of the penalty area)

'Hold the spot!'

'Level with the 6!' (-yard box)

'Level with the ball!'

A word of caution. The keeper should never shout 'Leave it!' or 'Let it run!' without either prefixing it with the word 'Keeper's!' or by naming the teammate involved, for example, 'Keeper's, let it run!' or 'Leave it, John!' Failure to follow this advice could result in the referee penalising the goalkeeper for unsporting behaviour.

It is worth making the distinction between 'stepping up' and 'squeezing up' when exhorting the defence to push up after making a clearance. The object of pushing up is not necessarily to catch opponents offside, but to make play compact and reduce the amount of space and time available to the opposition. If the clearance falls to an opponent, the defence should push out gradually and then only if the ball carrier is put under pressure. This is to prevent the opponents from rebounding the ball back into the danger area behind the defence. If the clearance forces the opposition to turn and chase the ball or falls to a teammate in a forward position, the defence can push up quickly as there is little immediate danger of being caught out by an early pass to the back of the defence.

The purpose of holding the line is to make play compact and predictable but it cannot be done effectively unless the ball carrier is pressurised. The point at which the defence holds the line should make it difficult for the opponents to play a quality ball in behind the defence. Care must be taken that the line is not held too high as it will make it relatively easy for the opposition to play a penetrative pass. Whenever the defence holds the line, the keeper's voice should be heard and he should also be prepared to adopt an advanced starting position from which he can intercept passes played beyond it.

How

All information must be given in a loud, clear voice that instils confidence. Even if the goalkeeper feels nervous he should try to exude calm. He will achieve this if he provides early and relevant information in a confident and controlled manner. The gravity of the situation will determine the intonation of the instruction. For example, the call of 'Man on!' should convey urgency whereas 'Time, two-touch!' should induce composure on the part of the teammate.

The keeper should not forget to congratulate colleagues when they have performed well, but lambasting defenders is rarely beneficial and, in fact, probably disrupts concentration.

Nearly half of the goals at the highest level are scored from set plays

Given that so many goals are conceded from set pieces, the simplest solution is to avoid giving away any throw-ins, corners or free kicks in the defensive third of the field! Since this is unlikely, it is essential that teams develop effective strategies for defending set pieces. There are three elements that underpin successful defence in these situations.

Preparation and organisation

All teams should rehearse in training an agreed procedure when a set piece is conceded. To leave the organisation to chance may result in confusion and hand the initiative to the opposition. Since the idea is to prevent the opposition from exploiting the set piece, all players should know beforehand how their team will respond in any given situation. This will entail instructing certain players to fulfil specific roles.

Individual responsibility

The best-laid plans will be rendered useless unless individual players carry out the jobs to which they have been assigned. On those occasions when team organisation may be weakened (following a substitution for example), it is important that another player takes responsibility for filling the breach in the defensive formation.

Concentration

Lapses of concentration can prove disastrous even before the ball is delivered. As soon as the set play is conceded, the team should take up their defensive positions. Trigger phrases such as 'When the ball is dead, be alive' will help players to keep on their toes.

The defensive organisation at set plays should be carefully thought out with the appropriate players chosen for the various jobs. It should also be constantly drilled during training sessions with reinforcement given before each game. Some coaches use diagrams stuck to the dressing room wall as a means of reminding the players of their responsibilities. When the opposition's strengths and weaknesses are known to the coach, he may choose to amend the set piece organisation to counteract a specific threat. However, it is usually a good idea to give players regular jobs because this will enhance concentration.

DEFENDING THROW-INS

The short throw

As the ball is being retrieved, the defenders should move quickly into defensive positions. Opponents who constitute the greatest threat should be marked first. Each defender in the vicinity of the throw should mark goal-side at a distance of 2–3 yards, forming a triangle between himself, the opponent and the ball. In this position he will be able to cover a sharp movement by his opponent and also make up ground to challenge should the ball be thrown to his attacker. When the opponent receives the ball, the defender should put him under heavy pressure to make control difficult and to prevent him from turning. In addition, another defender should be deployed in the space between the nearest attacker and the ball, so that high-quality service back to the thrower is denied and so the thrower is marked once he enters the field of play. (See Figure 53.)

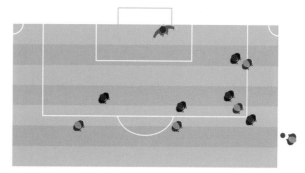

Figure 53 Defending short throw-ins

Defenders well away from the action do not have to mark so tightly since they have a responsibility for covering teammates and key areas of space as well as looking after their opponent. The goalkeeper should be in the front half of the goal.

The long throw

The long throw can be quite a potent weapon because the trajectory of the ball is usually fairly low and does not allow the keeper much time to deal with it. Defenders can anticipate that opponents are preparing to use the long throw tactic because they usually position a tall target player in the area between the near post and the junction of the 6-yard box. Rather than heading directly for goal, this player will be aiming to flick the ball on for teammates in the space behind him. Once the ball has been flicked on, the defence has a problem.

Defensive arrangements should be made to reduce the potency of the throw and to prevent the target player gaining the vital first touch. A defender should stand in front of the thrower to force him to steepen the trajectory of the throw. The higher the trajectory, the longer the ball will be in the air and the more time the defence has to deal with the situation. The normal marking organisation should apply, with the exception of marking in front and behind the opponents' target player. Where possible defenders should mark according to size.

If the attacker does make the flick-on, the defence should then deal with the 'second ball' which is likely to travel 2–6 yards behind the target player. (See shaded area in Figure 54.) Defenders should be ready to cover this area to prevent any secondary chances.

The higher, full-length throw might afford time for the keeper to deal with the first ball. However, if the delivery is shorter and lower into the congested area in front of the near post, the keeper should resist the temptation to attack and deal with the flick-on instead.

DEFENDING CORNERS

Often a subject of much debate, there is no foolproof defensive arrangement when defending corners. There are two basic tactics employed in defending corners: man-to-man or zonal marking. My preference is a combination of the two as it delegates specific areas of responsibility to defenders and the goalkeeper as well as providing the opportunity to cover the opposition's most dangerous players. However, it must be stressed that, as in many cases, the end has to justify the means, and if a team has a system for defending corners that is consistently successful, then they should not tamper with it. It is essential that all players are comfortable with the agreed organisation and, more importantly, believe in it.

The purpose of set piece defensive planning is to make it as difficult as possible for the opposition to score, so it is vital that the team is well drilled and briefed on both individual responsibilities and general organisation. There will be occasions in matches when, due to substitutions, key players will be missing and those players remaining on the field of play will have to display the presence of mind to plug the gaps. This speed of thought may also be required when players are 'dragged' out of position by the movement of opponents.

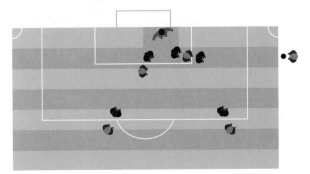

Figure 54 Defending long throw-ins

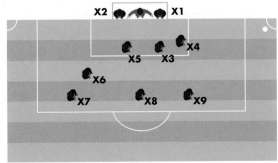

Figure 55 Defending corners

The corner played into the near post is the most difficult to defend, so it is important that this area is well manned. (See Figure 55.) One player (X1) covers the near post while two other defenders (X3 and X4) mark the space in front of the 6-yard box. Other defenders are stationed at the back post (X2) and at the rear of the 6-yard box (X5). The three players marking the 6-yard box are responsible for the space in front of them and it is important that they are fairly tall and good headers of the ball. The goalkeeper takes care of high balls delivered into the 6-yard box and the two defenders on the post cover the keeper when he leaves his line. Two of the team's smaller players should guard the area between the 6-yard box and the edge of the penalty area to mop up partial clearances. The remaining players should be asked to mark according to size.

It is a good idea to leave at least two of the team's best headers (X6 and X7) to pick up the opposition's dangermen. If the opponents play a short corner, it is important that the zonal markers resist moving out of position and leave the task of pressurising the kick to the shorter players who are marking the space towards the edge of the box. If, in an emergency, any of the zonal players is to be drawn out of position, it should be the defender guarding the near post because his role is not as critical as those patrolling the front of the 6-yard box. It must also be remembered that when the short corner is played, it requires two defenders to counter a 1 v 2 situation.

When opponents take up positions for a near-post corner, it is crucial that defenders mark in front of the first player and behind the last. The object of the exercise is to prevent the ball from being flicked on. This situation presents some difficult decision making for the keeper – should he attack the corner and risk being beaten by the flick-on? Or does he allow the defenders to deal with it and intercept the flick-on if it occurs?

Generally speaking, if the trajectory is flat and the defenders are best placed to clear the danger, the keeper should maintain his mid-goal position and prepare to deal with the second ball. On the other hand, if the corner is flighted without much pace and is above the heads of the crowd at the near post, he may have sufficient space and time to claim the ball. In this case, experience is the best teacher, but the keeper will be well advised

to treat each situation on its own merits and not to commit himself until he has assessed the flight and pace of the ball.

If the opposition sends players deep into the 6-yard box, the keeper should not allow his own players to mark them. To do so would congest his area even further. The keeper must back his ability to beat opponents in the air, if not with a catch then at least with a punch. The zonal markers will deal with the danger if the opponent pulls off the line and out of the 6-yard box. One advantage of zonal marking is that by delegating areas of responsibility, decision making becomes easier. Moreover, the further the opposition is from goal when they meet the ball, the less chance there is of a goal being conceded.

Defending free kicks around the penalty area

Free kicks conceded in and around the penalty area will necessitate forming a defensive wall to cover the part of the goal nearest to the ball. Guided by the defensive principle of making play predictable, the wall discourages opponents from shooting directly at the nearest part of the goal. The goalkeeper, who should be positioned in the half of the goal not masked by the wall (so that he can see the ball), will happily deal with shots aimed in his direction because he is only covering part of the goal. (See photo 74.)

Figure 74 Goalkeeper's position at free kicks

When a free kick is conceded close to the penalty area the goalkeeper should ask himself the following questions:

• Do I need a wall?

• Where should it be positioned?

• How many players should be in the wall?

The number of players in the wall is determined by the position of the free kick. (See Figure 56.) Generally speaking, the nearer and more central the free kick, the greater the number of players in the wall. As the distance of the free kick from the goal increases, the number of players in the wall decreases. Excessive numbers should not be used in the wall as it reduces the number of players available to carry out marking jobs, and it gives the keeper less chance to see the ball.

All teams should have a defensive plan for dealing with free kicks. It is useful to give players positions in the wall. As defenders are usually more adept in marking, the wall is best left to designated midfield players.

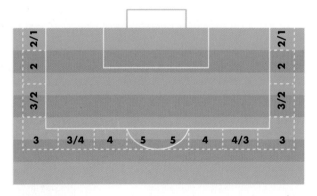

Figure 56 Number of players in the defensive wall

As soon as the free kick is awarded, the keeper should organise his defence according to the rehearsed strategy. Skilful players will attempt to take the kick while the keeper is preoccupied with lining up the wall, so it is vitally important that the organisation is slick and takes as little time as possible. (Allowing outfield players to line up the wall requires considerable skill so it is recommended that the keeper, who is obviously in a better position to do so, takes that responsibility.)

The goalkeeper points out which side the wall should cover and decides on the number of players in it. It is best to have the taller players at the near post side in order to prevent the kicker dipping the ball over the end of the wall. The keeper lines up his end player with the near post and then instructs him to take a step sideways in order to prevent a shot being curled around the edge of the wall. Instructions should be clear and concise such as 'Move two yards to the right. Stop!' It is imperative that the goalkeeper does not stand behind the wall and thus obscure his view of the ball. With this arrangement, the keeper can prepare himself to receive a direct shot in his half of the goal. If the ball is chipped over or bent around the wall it will not be hit with pace and, therefore, will give the keeper time to move across and save. The keeper should not gamble and move before the ball is struck. Too many goals are scored because the keeper, in anticipating a shot over or around the wall, has moved early and been beaten in the part of the goal he was supposed to be covering. It must be remembered that brilliant creative play will overcome the best defensive strategy so, if the keeper is beaten by an outstanding strike, he should not be blamed if the organisation was as good as it could be. Generally if the free kick is awarded on the edge of the penalty area it is highly unlikely that the kicker will have sufficient space to play the ball over or around the wall. In these situations he will invariably shoot powerfully at the nearest part of the goal, towards the area where the keeper should be positioned.

Occasionally, the kicker will tap the ball inside to increase the shooting angle for another player. To counter this there should be a defensive 'charger' a yard or so off the end of the wall, who will quickly pressurise the ball if it is played sideways. (See player X in Figure 57.) The keeper should adjust his position accordingly when the ball is played sideways. Other defenders should be used to mark opponents elsewhere in the area.

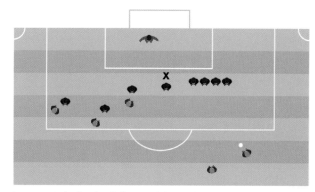

Figure 57 Defending free kicks around the penalty area

For free kicks in wider positions, the wall will not only prevent a direct shot but will also deny the kicker the opportunity to drive in a low cross. As the player will be forced to loft the ball the keeper can take up a position to defend the cross. The increased height on the ball will give the defence more time to clear the danger.

For those indirect free kicks conceded inside the area, it will be necessary to pull all players back to defend. If the kick is awarded within 10 yards of the goal, it is advisable to have a six- or seven-player wall with the keeper in the middle. As soon as the kick is taken the keeper should converge on the ball with the intention of blocking the shot. Spare defenders should be used to mark opponents in the penalty area. (See Figure 58.)

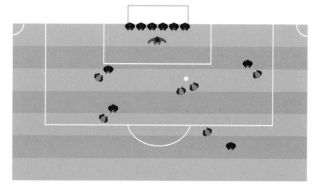

Figure 58 Free kicks inside the penalty area

Practices for defending throw-ins, corners and free kicks

These practices can take place in attack versus defence situations or in an 11-a-side game. The coach can either wait until throw-ins, corners or free kicks occur naturally, or award them arbitrarily throughout the game.

Key points

- Staying alert when the set piece has been conceded. Take up defensive positions quickly as the ball is being retrieved.
- Clear, loud and decisive instructions from the keeper followed by rapid and calm organisation.
- Awareness of individual and collective responsibilities.
- If the ball is played into the penalty the defenders should aim to be first to the ball.
- Be ready to contest the second ball.
- Be aware of counter-attacking possibilities.

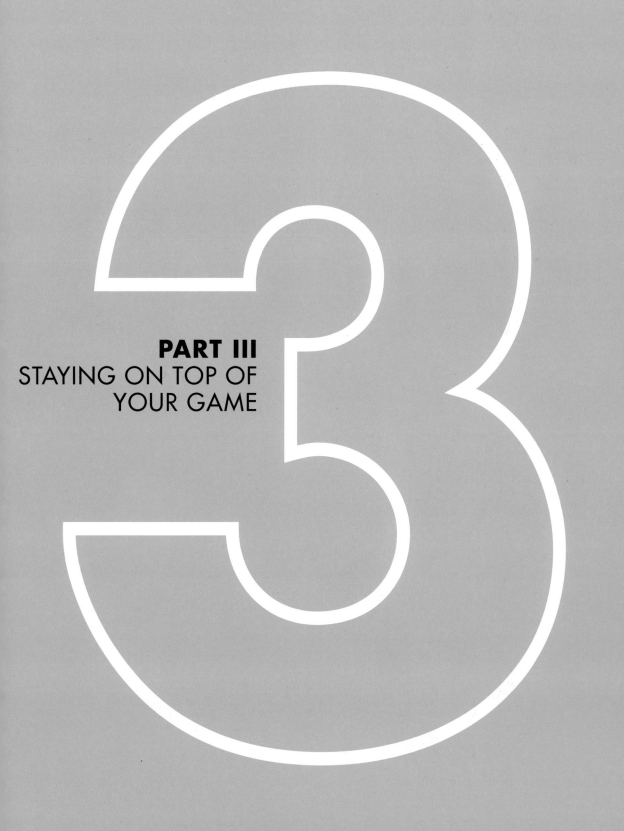

PART III
STAYING ON TOP OF
YOUR GAME

TOP TIPS FOR PLAYING IN FIVE-A-SIDE AND FUTSAL

22

Playing in small-sided game formats can do much to polish the keeper's reactions and distribution skills

Aside from the rules, the main difference between playing in the 11 v 11 game and the five-a-side and futsal formats is that there is less time and space available in the small-sided game versions. Having to defend smaller goals means that physique is not as important as having good reactions and being quick off and across the ground. In terms of the five goalkeeping roles, both formats create quicker passages of play where the goalie requires good close range shot-stopping and distribution skills.

However, despite having the same number of players and similar sized pitches, there are fundamental differences between five-a-side and futsal. In five-a-side the goals are typically 16 × 4 feet whereas for futsal they are 10 × 7 feet and this has significant implications for shot stopping techniques. In five-a-side where play is restricted below head height, the goalie should take up a low ready position and be prepared to use the collapsing or low diving save to reach ground shots. In futsal, diving is not recommended as opponents can shoot from inside the goal area. The keeper is advised to stay upright and use a range of blocking techniques involving the hands, torso, legs or feet to save the ball.

Another major difference is in the rules relating to leaving the goal area. In five-a-side the keeper is much more reactive and cannot leave his area and is mainly seen as a saver of shots and a thrower of the ball. However, in futsal he has unlimited access and, at times, is expected to play as a fifth player in joining in attacking play. The futsal goalie should therefore have well-developed receiving and passing skills, attributes that elite 11 v 11 goalkeepers should possess. The influence of the futsal four-second rule on perfecting scanning and distribution skills (particularly as part of a counter-attack) also cannot be ignored. Dealing with through balls is also a feature of futsal and the best keepers are adept at reading the game.

In both formats the keeper is expected to be a good thrower of the ball, particularly in javelin and sling techniques. Surrendering possession close to goal can prove disastrous in both formats so quick, accurate and well-weighted throws from the goalkeeper are essential.

In assessing the transfer of skills from the small-sided to the 11 v 11 version of the game, there is no doubt that futsal has more value than five-a-side. Goalkeepers who have played futsal in their youth tend to be very comfortable with the ball at their feet, have a good grasp of counter-attacking, and are excellent blockers and savers with their feet and legs.

Rather than list bespoke practices for five-a-side and futsal (many of which are similar to those described earlier in the book), this chapter provides useful tips for the two small-sided games.

GOALKEEPING IN FIVE-A-SIDE

Shot Stopping
- Constantly adjust your position as the ball moves so that you are always in the right place as the opponent shoots; and always be ready.

- Adopt a low ready position and become an expert in the collapsing and low diving saves.

- If not making a clean catch, parry or deflect into safety zones (wide of the goal).

- Develop sharp reactions for dealing with close-range shots.

Distribution
- On catching the ball, look to distribute before the opposition is organised.

- Identify the most penetrative player who can receive the ball with comfort before choosing the appropriate throwing technique (roll, javelin or sling).

- Counter-attack to advantage. If counter-attacking, throw to the back foot (the one closest to the opponent's goal) and if seeking to retain possession throw to the safe side.

GOALKEEPING IN FUTSAL

Shot Stopping
- Develop a full range of blocking techniques.

- Stay big and avoid diving for low shots.

- Recover quickly to make second saves.

- Become proficient at deflecting wide of the goal.

- Develop good reactions and do not panic when unsighted.

- Saving in 1 v 1 situations happens frequently in futsal so practise closing down the opponent quickly and executing the most appropriate blocking technique.

- With the low bounce ball and tight spaces, be light on the feet and cover the ground quickly.

Distribution
- On receiving the ball, scan quickly and understand the value of counter-attacking.

- Perfect the javelin and low-sling throwing techniques.

- Work hard on outfield skills.

- Understand when to leave the area to create 5 v 4 scenarios.

Dealing with through balls
- Become a good reader of the game and a good judge of the through ball.

The demands of the modern game necessitate specific physical conditioning for the goalkeeper

Fitness training, like coaching, is a means to an end. Unless it results in improving match performance, it is pointless. Players who wish to fulfil their potential must ensure that they are fully equipped to meet the demands of the modern game. To put it another way, players should not be able to blame poor preparation for a substandard performance. The importance of a comprehensive coaching programme and pre-match warm-up has already been covered, but this will be negated if players are not physically capable of sustaining a desirable level of performance. Consequently, the coach should be aware of the fitness needs of all of his players.

Reaching peak fitness and then maintaining it is not easy and it is not without its share of discomfort. There is a saying, 'No pain, no gain', which contains a large element of truth. Players must work hard in training throughout the season because fitness is not like a bank account that accrues interest when left alone. It must be constantly topped up or the level will diminish. The key to maintaining fitness is motivation. If training is enjoyable, purposeful and competitive, players will be motivated to push themselves ensuring that fitness levels benefit. Since fitness is so important, the coach must not approach the subject haphazardly. The whole programme should be carefully planned. The intensity and frequency of fitness training must be related to individual needs, which in turn are determined by the age, physical development and performance level of the players involved.

The fitness requirements of the goalkeeper are not the same as an outfield player as the demands of the position are different. Keepers need to have quick feet and a good spring, but also the upper body strength to cope with the hardest of shots and the strongest

Other considerations include:

- TIMING and FREQUENCY. It is likely that the most intensive work will take place during the pre-season training period. Subsequent fitness sessions throughout the year will be aimed at maintaining levels. Care should be taken that intensive work does not take place too close to matches because performance may be impaired.

- INTENSITY and VARIETY. A varied training programme based on quality rather than quantity of work is the preferred option. There is a danger that the goalkeeper can over train and do too much on the training field. In the short term it can impair match performance and in the long term make him vulnerable to injury.

- MONITORING. The regular, objective monitoring of fitness during training sessions can be achieved reliably via time trials, circuit training and so on.

- EVALUATION. The regular, subjective evaluation of the fitness programme and how it impacts on match performance is crucial.

of physical challenges. In addition, they ought to possess the suppleness and speed of reaction to deal with the unexpected. All of these qualities need to be founded upon a good level of cardiovascular fitness.

In order to make the work realistic and enjoyable a ball should be used as much as possible. However, it is imperative that the coach appreciates the difference between coaching and training. Many people wrongly assume that goalkeeping coaching is pressure training (rapid repetitions of a particular exercise). Skill levels will break down once fatigue sets in, so when coaching a particular technique, the keeper needs time to digest the key factors if he is to carry out the practice successfully. With pressure training, there is little time for such reflection and within a few minutes the player is too exhausted to perform the technique in the desired manner. Pressure training has its uses in improving endurance and strength, but not in the perfection of technique.

Coaches must ensure that the training is appropriate for the players involved. For younger players the emphasis should be on enjoyment and the mastery of technique with any fitness benefits being incidental. However, for goalkeepers working at the elite level it is recommended that supervised basic core strength training and conditioning should commence from the age of 12 years. As players mature physically, the specific fitness demands (including degree of difficulty, number of sets and repetitions) will increase. There are many excellent fitness specific books on the market that will provide a more comprehensive range of exercises than this one. This chapter will cover drills that require minimal equipment and are relatively easy to organise.

Four fitness areas for goalkeepers are identified and a selection of exercises for each is provided below. As the list is by no means exhaustive the coach should use his imagination to keep the sessions relevant, varied and fresh. Working with a ball will help to maintain motivation levels. It is recommended that, with the exception of speed and agility work, fitness drills occur towards the end of sessions once the technical/tactical aspects have been covered.

ENDURANCE
The goalkeeper should not be excused from running drills involving outfield players, but exercises should be tailored to suit the goalkeeper's needs given the uniqueness of the position.

(1) The barrage
Organisation
A number of balls are spread out in an arc around the goalmouth (10 yards from the goal line). Starting at one end, the server shoots in rapid succession. The keeper has to save as many shots as possible. (See Figure 59.) After a brief rest (3:1 rest to work ratio) the exercise is repeated with the keeper trying to improve his previous score. The server may wish to vary the distance of the shots depending on the goalkeeper's needs. It is vitally important that the service is tailored to the ability of the keeper. Sufficient time between each shot must be allowed so that good technique is maintained throughout. In other words, the keeper must be given the chance to save. Merely blasting every shot into the back of the net will demotivate the keeper and afford very little benefit.

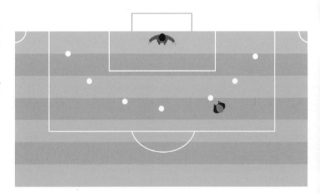

Figure 59 The barrage

(2) The Corrigan
Organisation
This exercise is named after the former Manchester City and England goalkeeper Joe Corrigan, who included it as part of his daily training routine. Two servers stand level with a post 6–7

yards from the goal, armed with four balls each. One server feeds the ball low towards the post so that the keeper is forced to make a diving save. As he gets up, the second server feeds high towards the other post. The keeper has to move quickly to save. This process is repeated until all the balls have been used. This exercise is extremely demanding and the goalkeeper should be given sufficient rest before repeating it. For more advanced performers, the number of balls can be increased. (See Photo 75 sequence)

(3) The shuttle

Organisation

This exercise involves three goals – two 5-yard goals located 15 yards from the goal line on each side of the goal, and a full-size goal. (See Figure 60.) The keeper, starting from his near post, approaches goal A and server 1 (S1) forces him to make a sharp save. The keeper has to recover immediately and look to save from S2 shooting at goal B. He then touches the far post and approaches goal C to make another sharp save from S3. The keeper has one final shot to save from S2 aiming for goal B. The exercise is repeated five times (with 3:1 rest to work ratios) and is conducted at high speed.

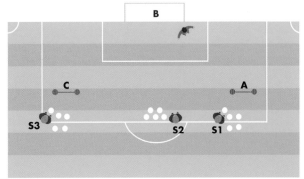

Figure 60 The shuttle

Photo 75 sequence The Corrigan

(4) The circuit

Organisation

The goalkeeper sprints 12 yards to two balls placed 1 yard apart. He completes 15 press-ups with his hands on top of the balls. He sprints back to the start, completes a forward roll, turns and sprints out to another ball 15 yards from the line. The keeper dives flat onto his stomach and the coach throws the ball into the air. The keeper has to leap to his feet and catch the ball at the highest safest point. This is repeated 10 times. He then sprints back to the line, completes a forward roll, turns and sprints out to another ball 18 yards away. Here the goalkeeper lies flat on his back and the server throws the ball so that the keeper has to sit up to catch. This is repeated 30 times. The keeper sprints back to the line, completes a forward roll and then rests. Advanced performers can attempt two or three circuits without rest. Younger players can complete each circuit with a 3:1 rest to work ratio in between. (See Figure 61.) In order to monitor progress, the coach could record the time taken to complete the circuit(s).

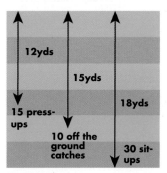

Figure 61 The circuit

(5) Continuous collapsing saves

Organisation

The keeper starts at one end of the goal area with the server standing 4–6 yards away. The server plays the ball along the ground forcing the goalkeeper to make a collapsing save. Having made the save, the keeper rolls the ball back as he gets to his feet. The server returns the ball so that the goalkeeper makes another collapsing save. This process continues until the other end of the goal area is reached at which point the exercise continues in the opposite direction. Three return journeys are completed before resting. The server must control the pace of the practice so that the keeper has sufficient time to perform the save correctly.

(6) Continuous low diving saves

Organisation

Similar to (5) but the server and the keeper work over a 40-yard area. The server throws the ball to the side of the keeper at waist height. Having executed a low diving save, the keeper immediately returns the ball to the server who moves on a step and serves again. Once the keeper arrives at the end of the course he rests before making the return journey, this time diving to the other side.

SPEED/MOBILITY

When engaged in speed training it is very important that the goalkeeper works at maximal effort and is allowed to fully recover between exercises.

(1) Square sprinting

Organisation

The goalkeeper starts in the middle of a 10-yard square with balls placed in each corner. On the command he sprints out to the corner, touches the ball, turns, returns to the middle, touches the ball and then moves off to another corner. This process is repeated until each ball has been touched. Rest to work ratios should be at least 5:1. On subsequent exercises the type of running required can be varied, for example, forward out and backwards back to the middle, or sideways out and sideways back. (See photo 76.)

Photo 76 Square sprinting

(2) Short sprinting

Organisation

This exercise is best conducted with two or more players performing at the same time to create a competitive situation. The keeper lies or sits 5 yards from the ball. On the command he has to rise and gather the ball as quickly as possible. The coach may vary the starting position and the distance to be covered. Once again the rest to work ratio should be 5:1.

(3) Off the ground to save

Organisation

The goalkeeper lies or kneels 12 yards from the goal line facing his own goal. The server standing 5–10 yards away at an angle plays the ball towards goal. On the command from the server the keeper has to rise and move quickly to prevent the ball from crossing the line. (See Figure 62.)

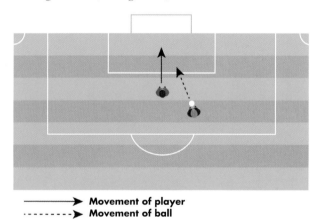

⎯⎯⎯▶ **Movement of player**
‑ ‑ ‑ ‑ ‑ ‑ ▶ **Movement of ball**

Figure 62 Off the ground to save

(4) Quick pick-ups

Organisation

The keeper stands at one end of a 10-yard grid. The server throws the ball into the grid, and the keeper has to pick it up before the second bounce. (See Figure 63.)

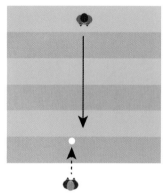

Figure 63 Quick pick-ups

AGILITY/FLEXIBILITY

(1) Forward roll

Organisation

With the ball in his hands, the goalkeeper completes a forward roll and returns to the feet in one movement. The exercise is repeated 6 times.

(2) Gliding on the backside

Organisation

The goalkeeper sits on the floor and the server feeds the ball to alternate sides. After each save the goalkeeper must thrust himself forwards without using his hands. Rhythmic feeding by the server will help the keeper move his trunk from the goal line to the edge of the penalty area.

(3) Avoiding the ball

Organisation
The goalkeeper lies on his back with two servers 3 yards either side of him. One server rolls the ball towards the keeper, who has to take evasive action so that it carries on unimpeded to the other server. The keeper can let the ball pass through by sitting up, arching his back or lifting his legs. The exercise is repeated 20 times. (See photos 77a and 77b.)

Figure 77a and 77b Avoiding the ball

STRENGTH

(1) Spring exercises

Organisation
Using a series of five hurdles or balls, the goalkeeper has to bounce over each obstacle. The keeper should use a variety of take-offs – bunny hops, left-leg hops, and right-leg hops. He should aim to achieve maximum spring over each obstacle. Care should be taken that the surface is not too hard to prevent joint injuries. There should be plenty of rest between each set. (See photo 78.)

Photo 78 Spring exercises

(2) Off the ground and spring

Organisation

The keeper takes a variety of positions on the ground. On the command the server throws the ball into the air and the goalkeeper has to rise quickly and jump to catch it. Repeat 10 times. In order to develop greater spring the keeper should be encouraged not to use their hands when getting up from his back or side.

(3) Rise to back pedal to save

Organisation

The keeper sits on the 6-yard line with the sever standing on the penalty spot. On the command the server throws the ball towards the goal. The keeper has to rise without the help of his hands, back pedal quickly and jump to catch the ball. Repeat 10 times.

(4) Abdominal exercises

Organisation

There are a number of exercises that can be used to develop abdominal strength.

- Sitting on the ground the goalkeeper has to catch balls delivered rapidly to alternate sides by the server standing 2–3 yards away. Twenty serves to each side.

- Sitting on the ground, with his knees bent, the goalkeeper lies with the ball in his hands. He lifts his lower back from the ground to touch his knees with the ball. Repeat 20 times.

- As in the exercise above but as the keeper rises he twists his trunk to touch the ball on the outside of his right knee. In the next sit-up he touches the outside of his left knee. Ten repetitions for each side.

- The keeper lies on his back with a ball resting on one hand. With his knees bent he slowly lifts his lower back from the ground. Hold for 5–10 seconds before slowly lowering to the ground. Repeat 5 times with the ball in each hand. Progress to raising the right leg when the ball is in the right hand. Repeat for the left side.

(5) Press-ups

Organisation

A choice of one of the following should be carried out at least three times per week.

- Ordinary press-ups (3 × 25).
- Press-ups on the knuckles (3 × 25).
- Press-ups on the fingers (3 × 15).
- Press-ups on two balls (3 × 10). (See photo 79.)
- Press-ups on one ball (3 × 10). (See photo 80.)
- 1 press-up, clap hands; 2 press-ups, clap hands; 3 press-ups, clap hands, and so on up to 10 press-ups.
- Press-up with one hand on the ball and one hand on the ground. After each press-up shift the ball to the other hand and repeat (3 × 10). Obviously, the number of press-ups will relate to the age and level of the performer, but the volume should increase over time.

Photo 79 Press up on two balls

Photo 80 Press up on one ball

The name of the game is keeping the ball out of the net

ADVICE FOR THE COACH

The aim of goalkeeping is to keep the ball out of the net, and if the keeper manages to do this safely and consistently using unorthodox techniques his 'style' must not be coached out of him. The purpose of this handbook is to help the goalkeeper carry out his job effectively, not to attain marks for artistic merit. So, if a keeper's method is successful game after game, the coach should not attempt to change it. My advice to youngsters is to observe and appreciate the top goalkeepers, but be wary of imitating them. Young players should develop their own style based on an awareness of their own strengths and limitations.

It is irritating when people discount promising young goal-keepers because they are 'too small'. Teenagers grow at different rates and a below-average sized goalkeeper at 11 years of age may be considerably taller than his peers by the age of 18. Furthermore, all keepers have their strengths and weaknesses, and a short player's strong points might be a taller player's failings. If the goalkeeper is performing well, making few errors, his height will not be an important factor. Since the coach can do little about genetics, he should concentrate on 'controlling the controllables' and helping his promising young players to fulfil their potential.

This is not to say that at senior level physique is not important. Over the last ten years it would appear that the average height of goalkeepers at the highest level has risen from about 6'2" to 6'4". There is a well-known cliché in soccer that 'A big good 'un is always better than a small good 'un', and this is true at professional level where the physical demands of the game can be very intense.

In recognising that the goalkeeper occupies the single-most important position in the team, the head coach should ensure that the keeper is given sufficient time in which to practise his craft. Merely completing a training session with a shooting drill will not satisfy a keeper's needs. He should have a personalised coaching programme based on the 'five goalkeeping roles' with specific emphasis on polishing his strengths and minimising his weaknesses. As far as the specialist coach is concerned, the goalkeeper must come first when planning sessions.

Tailoring the session to the goalkeeper's needs

All training sessions should incorporate some work on the basics of head, hands and feet as this reinforces confidence and the technical foundation on which the game is based. In addition, the coach should be able to identify areas of concern from match play, and should then organise sessions which concentrate on those aspects so that any faults can be rectified. The coaching session, which should be based on one or more of the five goalkeeping roles, should begin at a level where the keeper experiences some success before progressing to increasingly realistic practice situations. This progression from the easy to the difficult will help improve the keeper's confidence as well as his competence.

Good quality service

Poor feeding starves the practice, and progress will only be made if the keeper has lots of contact with the ball. The service should be challenging and attempt to bring out the best in the goalkeeper. If it is too easy, training will become boring, and conversely, if the keeper is constantly retrieving the ball from the back of the net, motivation levels will drop.

Outfield practice

Given that so much of the goalkeeper's work is with his feet, it is a useful exercise to allow him to be an outfield player in the development of possession practices and small-sided games. It will improve receiving and passing skills as well as developing better game understanding. The modern keeper must be comfortable with the back pass and dealing with the ball when he has to leave the area and the only way he is going to be proficient in these aspects is through regular practice.

Boosting morale

It is important that players enjoy their soccer. The coach can encourage this by making training sessions purposeful, stimulating and productive with the emphasis on enjoyment through improvement. Adhering to the premise that praise is a stronger motivating agent than criticism, the coach should ensure that the keeper leaves the training field confident in his ability and fully prepared for the next match. One way of doing this is to end every session with a save so that the keeper's self-esteem is left intact.

ADVICE FOR THE GOALKEEPER

Every goalkeeper, throughout the history of the game, has experienced at some time the utter despair of making mistakes that have cost crucial goals. Sometimes fate conspires to compound this misery so that the error affects the result of the game, or even the fortunes of a whole season. The 24 hours immediately after the game are the worst, when the goalkeeper constantly relives the incidents in his mind, longing for the next training session when he can exorcise the memories.

It is comforting to know that even the true greats of the game have visited this lonely place. However, it is how they come to terms with their mistakes that marks them out from the rest. Rather than let one mistake or poor performance damage confidence and herald a run of bad form, they put the mistake down to experience and work hard in training to ensure that it does not happen again. Furthermore, no one can turn back the clock, we can only deal with the present, and by adopting this philosophy, the keeper should be able to concentrate on the remainder of the match. Unless a goalkeeper can handle the pressure of dealing with mistakes he will never fulfil his potential.

Aside from developing this mental toughness, the goalkeeper owes it to himself and to his team to be in peak physical

To summarise, my final advice to the goalkeeper is encapsulated in the following 10 golden rules:

1. Master the art of goalkeeping. Goalkeeping is about excellent technique, mobility, reading the game and good decision making. Remember that the best make the difficult look easy.

2. Keep yourself in the best physical shape. To be a player at the highest level you have to be an athlete first.

3. Polish your strengths so that they stand out, work on your weaknesses so that they cannot be exploited.

4. Prepare thoroughly for every match including taking excellent care of your equipment.

5. Never let your standards drop or take things for granted. Complacency is the enemy of consistency. Respect the game and your opponent but be competitive especially with yourself. Always give your best in everything you do and let your talent make you a better person.

6. Learn to control situations, rather than letting them control you. Develop good communication skills and a presence on the pitch that takes charge of the penalty area. Be cool, calm and collected under pressure.

7. Stick up for yourself, don't become a scapegoat when the team goes through a bad patch.

8. Never lose faith in yourself. Fear can be a negative emotion so use it to keep you sharp and alert. Don't dwell on mistakes. Use them as learning tools to make you better. Always be positive.

9. Whenever your confidence is low go back to the basics.

10. Be humble, let your performances do the talking.

condition for match play. This will not only involve working hard in training but also approaching the game in the correct manner. All successful keepers have a single-minded determination to keep the ball out of the net. It is this commitment which drives them to practise hard and to perfect their craft. The keeper should also strive to cultivate an on-field personality that gives the impression that he is king of the penalty area and that he has everything under control. This will reinforce confidence in himself and his teammates.

In training, the keeper should concentrate on polishing technique and improving decision making. However, he should remember that there are occasions when application of the perfect technique is impossible and an untidy save is the only option. Moreover, the keeper must never lose sight of the fact that his job is to keep the ball out of the net, and if he mishandles a shot, he must make a second save. Many goalkeepers, angry at not making a clean catch, lose concentration after dropping the ball and fail to regain possession immediately. This can, of course, prove disastrous.

You're only as good as your next game

The good keeper will become a keen student of the game and be able to quickly analyse situations that develop in front of him. By understanding the roles and responsibilities of teammates as well as the capabilities of opponents, the goalkeeper will be able to read the game better and to identify and nullify threats before they become a problem. Above all, the keeper should try to be consistent. It is a useful analogy to equate good performances with a bank balance. When the goalkeeper plays well, he makes a deposit in his account, while performing poorly results in a withdrawal. Aiming to reach a predetermined number of deposits can motivate the keeper to perform well game after game.

Ironically, since the position in which they play is such a pressurised one, goalkeepers at the elite level find it difficult to enjoy the game while it is in progress. Therefore, the enjoyment tends to be retrospective. It is later on, when he has time to unwind and analyse his performance, that the keeper can look back on the game and his role in it with pride or disappointment. Generally speaking, an error-free game provides as much satisfaction as brilliant one-off saves. There is no better feeling than relaxing after a match reflecting upon a job well done.

PICTURE CREDITS

All incidental photos in the book © Gerard Brown, with the exception of photos 1–32, 34–38, 40–43, 45, 46, 51–58, 60–65, 67, 70–72 and 74–80, courtesy of the photographer from the first and second editions. Other photography: pages 7 © Emma Byrne; 8 and 159 © mooinblack/Shutterstock; 10, 24, 112, 138 and 170 © Maxisport/Shutterstock; 14 © Olga Dmitrieva/Shutterstock; 15 © muzsy/Shutterstock; 16 and 144 © Matthias Schrader/AP/PA Images; 23 © smileimage9/Shutterstock; 27 © Pukhov Konstantin; 32 © Natursports/Shutterstock; 38–39 © katatonia82/Shutterstock; 40 © Andrew Surma/Demotix/Demotix/PA Images; 44 © Claude Paris/AP/PA Images; 56 © Laszlo Szirtesi/Shutterstock; 62 © Stephen Pond/EMPICS Sport/PA Images; 68 and 154 © Herbert Kratky/Shutterstock; 74 © Bruno Fahy/Belga/PA Images; 79 and 122 © Adam Davy/Empics Sport/PA Images; 80 © Art Widak/Demotix/Demotix/PA Images; 86 © Sergei Grits/AP/PA Images; 94 © Daniel Ochoa de Olza/AP/PA Images; 96 © Alberto Lingria/Landov/PA Images; 97 © Alastair Grant/AP/PA Images; 98 © Nick Potts/PA Wire/PA Images; 110–111 © Rob Griffith/AP/PA Images; 114–115 © Jeff Roberson/AP/PA Images; 116 © Victor R. Caivano/AP/PA Images; 121 © Ted S. Warren/AP/PA Images; 134 © Tomasz Bidermann/Shutterstock; 147 © Bill Kostroun/AP/PA Images; 148 © Vlad1988/Shutterstock; 156 © Pal2iyawit/Shutterstock; 157 © photofriday/Shutterstock; 160 © Jonathan Hayward/The Canadian Press/PA Images; 168 © VI Images/PA Images.

INDEX